The World's Greatest Sporting Rivalries

By

Andrew O'Brien

&

Liam McCann

About the authors

Andrew O'Brien was born in Liverpool in 1976. After gaining his BA Honours degree in History he moved to London and spent six years at *The Daily Telegraph*. His first two books, *The Little Books of The Deadliest Catch* and *The Orient Express*, were released in 2012. Andrew is a lifelong Everton fan and plays golf off an unmentionable handicap. His books can be found at: http://goo.gl/W9gsg

Liam McCann was born in 1973. He gained a Bachelor of Arts degree in Sports Physiology & Psychology and excelled on the sports field, becoming county champion in three of the athletics field events. In 2003 he turned his hand to writing non-fiction sports and reference books. He has since had 15 published and is now working on an action / thriller series featuring Ed Sampson. His books can be found at: http://amzn.to/hdcDGY

Contents

Acknowledgements

It would not have been possible to write this book without contributions from many people, and we would particularly like to thank the sportsmen and women who gave us their valuable time: Dean Richards, Maggie Alphonsi, Daniel Ricciardo, Jean-Eric Vergne, Andy Whittall, Sam Gardner, Alan Smith, Tom Smith and Gary Street, and especially Peter Reid. We would also like to thank Clare Connell, Gavin McBride, Paul Nichol, Bryn Marshall and Toby Jenkins. And our special thanks go to Rich Glazier.

This book is dedicated to Betty, Martha, Selina and Sophie.

Introduction

What constitutes a great sporting rivalry? In writing this book we have tried to pick the finest head-to-heads, whether in the individual or team sports arena. We looked at the history of the contest, the personalities of the combatants, the implications and outcomes, and the impact on our national consciousness.

Selecting which rivalries to keep and those to discard was not easy. How, for example, do you decide on a footballing rivalry when you have so many great domestic clashes to choose from? With Rangers-Celtic, Spurs-Arsenal, Real Madrid-Barcelona, Boca Juniors-River Plate, Liverpool-Everton, the two Milan giants or Manchesters City and United, to name just a handful, you would find it extremely difficult to pick just one.

Instead, we opted for an international rivalry that has a long and troubled history, where the players are brought up to treat each other with contempt, and which is embedded on the national psyche of both countries. Through the rancour, however, the two have played some of the most sublime matches the international stage has ever seen.

Indeed, the history between two countries was always going to be a consideration when selecting the best team sports rivalries. Dean Richards, former England and Lions Number 8 and now coach of Newcastle Falcons, agrees. "We didn't need any extra motivation when facing the Scots, Irish or Welsh but we knew they were using the history between us as an incentive. That gave us all the motivation we needed, knowing that they were targeting the England game as their biggest of the Five Nations Championship. They would happily lose all their other games if it meant they could beat us."

The only time Richards felt extra pressure on a game was for the Grand Slam deciders or the knockout games in the World Cup. The press, naturally, hyped up the encounters but he preferred not to read about it because he felt it detracted from the team's preparation. Touring with the Lions was also a defining moment in a player's career, not because the games

7

were necessarily bigger than England matches but because the expectation was higher, and the media exposure more widespread.

Former Scotland and Lions prop Tom Smith agrees that the rivalry with England was felt the most keenly. "The games at Murrayfield were always a bit special, and the history between the teams was an important factor in the build-up. The media and fans hyped the game up and the intensity was definitely greater. It rubbed off on the players and made a win against England feel more special because you'd had to work so hard for it. However, if England played Scotland five times a year it would dilute the sense of occasion and importance, which can happen in club games.

"For that reason, our domestic matches didn't have the same media interest, although because of their proximity Leicester-Northampton fixtures were always special and the fans made it clear that this was the big one, the one they wanted to win most. Indeed, fans can play a huge role during the build-up to matches at any level. The opposing supporters on the 1997 Lions tour to South Africa played a big part in motivating us. I remember driving on the bus to Newlands in Cape Town. The fans had hung pictures of lions being strangled by springboks on the lampposts, and lines of South African supporters were showing their contempt for us. The fear of failure was almost overwhelming and we had to use that as motivation. Stephen Jones from *The Sunday Times* was quite negative about non-English selections (despite the fact that he is Welsh) and I was all too aware that two Irishmen and a Scot in the front row would take the blame if things went wrong. It may seem quite negative but sometimes fear of failure or fear of the consequences of failure can be extremely powerful. If you add it to the desire for success and the desire to win, however, you can use that pressure positively."

There is a comparison to be drawn between these Lions encounters and the England women's team when they play France or New Zealand. Maggie 'The Machine' Alphonsi has played more than 60 times for her country and always feels extra pressure when facing the French as there is usually so much riding on the result. "Every time we have played France it has been in a decider, either in a semi-final of the World Cup or in the final match of the Six Nations to decide who will be champion. The same goes for New Zealand. The rivalry that has developed between us has been based on the last three World Cup finals. Each time we have met them, they have beaten us. It is this history between the three teams that makes the rivalry so intense and unique. I try to use this added pressure positively so that I look forward to the match rather than fear it. I also like to make sure that I know the key individuals within the opposing squad. Before a big fixture I research and analyse the way they play and use these patterns to help structure the way I want to play, countering their game and imposing myself on the match. At domestic level, the inter-club rivalry feels different because there's more meaning to it. This is because you play your rivals many more times than what you would do at international level so the rivalry builds in intensity. And there is usually more history between you and your opposition at club level."

Former Arsenal and England striker Alan Smith found the same intensity was present during the build-up to big domestic derbies. "People on the street would mention it, the papers would be full of it and training would take on an extra edge. Everyone knew what this match meant to the fans so our manager would often use that in his team talk. Then motivation to do well wasn't a problem."

But things were often balanced on a knife edge if recent results and form were considered: "If we were playing well, you'd go into the game full of confidence. If not, there would be a bit of trepidation about. In general, even though there was more pressure on a derby, good players tended to handle it better than the average players. It was my job to find out about the strengths and weaknesses of my opposite number to try to gain an advantage. And I would be more confident and hold a psychological edge going into the contest if I had done well against that player previously."

Smith also believed that you could feel pressure from your team-mates, although, if he was scoring every week, he rarely worried about being replaced. Occasionally, however, the rivalry between players at the same club did lead to tension and the odd altercation, although it was generally healthy competition for a place in the starting XI rather than descending into fisticuffs.

There's no doubt that the best cricketing rivalries draw on the same emotions. India and Pakistan also have a long and fascinating cricketing history, for example, but the Ashes is arguably the sport's greatest prize. Zimbabwe's Andy Whittall felt that although the history between nations was a factor in the build-up to a game, he tried to minimise its impact and concentrate instead on knowing the opposition's strengths and weaknesses, using pressure positively and relying on his own technique – in short, concentrating on the professional aspects of playing the game without worrying too much about previous encounters. Although there was different intensity – and therefore a greater rivalry – at international level, he felt it was important to bring a professional approach to all matches.

Providing the rivals are relatively evenly matched, great personalities also contribute to spellbinding contests. Who can forget the epic on-court duels between Chris Evert and Martina Navratilova, or Bjorn Borg and John McEnroe in the late 1970s and early '80s? Throw in an element of danger and personal hatred and you have one of the most compelling rivalries in sporting history in the shape of Formula 1 giants Alain Prost and Ayrton Senna. They may have been team-mates at McLaren for two seasons but initial respect soon turned sour, and by 1989 the gloves were off.

For current Toro Rosso drivers Jean-Eric Vergne and Daniel Ricciardo, mutual respect and the sharing of information are two of the keys to success. As there is always pressure to succeed, Vergne feels that wanting to beat your team-mate is both natural and healthy, for the team and the sport in general, but there is no extra pressure to do so. He also feels that trust is a key element of the close racing of the lower formulae, as well as in F1.

"There might have been some days in Formula 3 when racing got quite difficult, but not in F1 now with Daniel as we have known each other for such a long time and we know we can race one another safely. In the lower formulae, even when we were in the same team, we were racing quite hard but we were always safe. He is someone I trust on and off the track and that makes him a good team-mate for me. If Daniel beats me, it gives me the incentive to train harder because it means he's doing something better than me."

Ricciardo agrees: "Your biggest rivalry is with your team-mate because he is the only driver with identical equipment and therefore the first person you aim to beat. I think you can sometimes put pressure on yourself to make sure you at least beat him. If he beats me, it gives me extra motivation, but it's certainly not the only reason to train harder. We've had some pretty intense battles but it's always been fair. You need to show respect, especially in F1, because it can be dangerous if you don't."

Putting aside the competitive but fair rivalry within the team, both men agree that their next targets are the teams around them boasting similar levels of performance: Force India, Williams and Sauber. Whereas Vergne prefers to concentrate on his own performance however, Ricciardo admits he does have one eye on who he feels he can beat from those rival teams.

Monitoring the opposition is also a factor for one of Britain's top off-road triathletes, Sam Gardner, although he'd rather concentrate on his own performance than spend too much time checking the form of his rivals: "With the advent of the internet it is very easy to check start lists and see exactly who is racing. It is also easy to check their previous results and work out if they are a strong swimmer or runner etc. Personally, I tend not to do this as it would be too easy to get het up on factors outside your control, such as their training routines and recent form. The bottom line is that I need to get all three disciplines to a level where I can finish in the shortest time. However, it is useful to know your competitors' strengths and weaknesses. I know that Ian Leitch is a strong runner and to beat him I need to have a minute or two in the bank coming off the bike. I wouldn't alter my training especially for him, but I might change tactics on the day if something isn't working. The financial benefits on offer for a professional racer put added pressure on me to do well, so I need to take every advantage I can."

No book on sporting rivalries would be complete without two of the greatest heavyweight boxers. Although they ended their careers with mutual respect, perhaps, through gritted teeth, even a little admiration, when Muhammad Ali and Joe Frazier climbed through the ropes it was as if they were going to war.

Rivals can also inspire one another to heights that they probably wouldn't have achieved had it not been for the competition. Steve Ovett and Sebastian Coe traded world middle-distance records for more than a decade, while decathletes Daley Thompson and Jürgen Hingsen did battle in the same period for the right to be called the 'world's greatest athlete'.

The contests don't always have to be about blood, guts and thunder, however – just ask chess grandmasters Fischer and Spassky – although in the case of Rugby League's State of Origin it certainly helps! The duel in the sun between golfers Jack Nicklaus and Tom Watson captured the imagination of the public and brought the country to a standstill, but we opted for the Golden Bear's rivalry with Arnold Palmer. Their unforgettable head-to-heads dominated golf for more than a decade and changed the face of the sport forever; without them, the game you see today would be immeasurably different.

Today, the Ryder Cup is one of sport's most compelling rivalries. No one watching will forget the epic final day in the 2012 contest at Medinah, for example. The European fight-back surely ranks as one of sport's greatest spectacles, and the climax of the match was genuinely nerve-shredding. This incredible finish served to underline why the world's greatest sporting rivalries are so utterly beguiling and why sports fans across the globe will always debate which duel is the greatest of them all.

With that in mind, here is our selection of the world's finest sporting rivalries.

Björn Borg

vs

John McEnroe

The 2008 Wimbledon men's final between Roger Federer and Rafael Nadal is thought by many to be the greatest grand slam final in history. In fact, some believe it to be the best tennis match in history, and with it the apogee of the fiercest rivalry the game has ever seen.

However, despite the nerve-wracking drama that the 2008 final and its protagonists – forgive the pun – served up, it doesn't yet have the privilege of hindsight to further raise the extraordinary drama to the level of a game played on the same court 28 years earlier.

Quite simply, the men's modern game had already witnessed a titanic final and rivalry infinitely more fascinating and unequivocally more deserving of its definitive status: Björn Borg versus John McEnroe or, as many called it, Fire versus Ice.

In this clash, the vastly different on-court personalities of the two combatants – one with a fuse shorter than Genghis Khan's, the other possessing a calm demeanour that would make the Fonz look flustered – suggested the possibility either of combustion or even complete meltdown.

Björn Borg was the brilliant baseliner from Sweden, eulogised as cool, unflappable and sexy. John McEnroe, meanwhile, was the sublime yet brash and volatile volleyer from the Big Apple. For three years their rivalry transcended tennis.

Borg was born in Södertälje on June 6th 1956, a

predominantly working-class city southwest of Stockholm. An only child, he had a less privileged upbringing than McEnroe, but once his talent emerged his parents did their best to nurture it.

It may be hard to believe but, as a youngster, it was in fact Borg not McEnroe who was the owner of a fierce temper. So, to keep his volatile nature in check he cultivated an ice-cool image that was actually at odds with a naturally hot temperament.

The 'Ice-Borg' mastered the art of masking his emotions, and by 1976, at the age of 20, he had won both the French and Wimbledon titles. He was the youngest ever winner of the French Open (a record that stood until fellow Swede Mats Wilander broke it in 1982) and a player of such grace that the great Ilie Năstase, who Borg beat convincingly in the 1976 Wimbledon final, once said about him, "We're playing tennis, and he's playing something else."

By 1978, his dominance of the men's game was absolute. But then along came a cocky upstart from New York City, who was to put a severe dent in Borg's comfortable lifestyle.

In many respects, McEnroe is the easier to analyse and understand of the two men. Born on February 16th 1959, McEnroe was raised in the borough of Queens in New York in a comfortable middle-class family. He attended prestigious private schools, had access to tennis clubs and, being the eldest of three boys, he was indulged.

A stubborn streak marked his personality, but he nevertheless rose quickly through the ranks of junior tennis. In 1977, the 18-year-old achieved his big breakthrough, unexpectedly reaching the semi-finals of Wimbledon.

Dressed in a replica of Borg's iconic Fila shirt, it was here that he caught his first glimpse of the reigning king of Wimbledon, and the teen worship that Borg inspired in hordes of young girls. Despite defeat in four sets to fellow American Jimmy Connors, the headstrong yet enthralling McEnroe had arrived.

However, everything was to change when Borg faced McEnroe for the first time in the semi-final of the Stockholm Open in the autumn of 1978, at a time when Borg had no real opponents.

He had been ranked number one in the world for more than two years and had amassed grand slam titles in London and Paris. Supported by a devoted Romanian girlfriend, Mariana Simionescu, and his coach Lennart Bergelin, and having earned enough in the way of prize money and endorsements to guarantee financial stability for life, Borg sat proudly on top the tennis world.

However, the seemingly imperious Swede was upset, 3–6, 4–6, in a match McEnroe called "the greatest moment of my career". And so tennis's greatest rivalry was born.

Borg lost to McEnroe again in four sets in the final of the 1979 WCT Finals but was now overtaking Jimmy Connors for the top ranking. He established himself firmly as the world's number one with his fourth French Open singles title and fourth straight Wimbledon singles title, defeating Connors in a straight-set semi-final in the latter.

At the season-ending Masters tournament in January 1980, Borg played McEnroe for a third time in a thrilling semi-final, and this time he had the measure of his new nemesis, finishing his campaign with a 6–7, 6–3, 7–6 victory. However, in six short months, this match would be eclipsed by an encounter that has entered folklore in SW19.

The 1980 Borg-McEnroe Wimbledon final possessed a supreme urgency, partly because everyone could sense a titanic struggle between two tennis players whose very identities were on the line.

The match was already destined to be the most memorable for years, but then came a tie-break the like of which may never be seen again. There have been longer Wimbledon tie-breaks, but it is the 34-point battle between Borg and McEnroe that will forever be remembered.

McEnroe had seven set points and Borg five match points, four on his own serve. Finally McEnroe took it, but at what a price. He later admitted he had been exhausted by the emotional and physical strain, while Borg, who always spent more time on the practice court than McEnroe, had enough left.

Borg looked demoralised, but after 14 more games, he would claim one of Wimbledon's great victories. The Swede conceded only three points on his seven service games in the fifth set and broke the American with yet another backhand pass to win the greatest match centre court has ever seen: 1-6, 7-5, 6-3, 6-7 (16-18), 8-6.

In some ways, though, this defeat was the making of McEnroe and the undoing of Borg. McEnroe was young and resilient enough to come back the following year and displace Borg, and the price of doing so was to set in motion the self-doubt that eventually led to Borg's shocking retirement.

For three years, McEnroe had given Borg a reason to rise to a level beyond his comfort zone, but having suffered defeat at the American's hands in the 1981 Wimbledon final, Borg saw himself facing McEnroe again in the US Open final in September 1981. This was to be their last competitive encounter.

McEnroe won in four sets and Borg walked off court without even bothering to appear for the presentation ceremony. The New York crowd booed, while reporters chased the grim-faced Swede to a waiting car, where he slid behind the wheel and drove himself away from Flushing Meadow. It was his last grand slam match.

Borg's skilful relentlessness – typified in the classic five-set marathon with McEnroe in 1980 that brought the Swede's fifth successive coronation – left no one in any doubt about how special he was. However, here he was now, a shadow of his former self. His career was effectively over at the age of just 25, and McEnroe was left with just one opponent: himself.

When he found out his great adversary was retiring from the game, McEnroe's response was one of utter disbelief. "It made absolutely no sense to me, none." And then, of course, panic. "I would ask him, 'When are you coming back? Tennis needs you. I need you.'"

With other opponents, McEnroe competed against his own potential, his own incredibly high expectations. But it was his immense respect for the Swede that allowed him to play him head-on and forget himself.

A forlorn McEnroe was alone now, and his loathing for this situation unleashed a new flood of fury, indulging in behaviour which Borg described as "berserk. Like a mental patient they just released".

McEnroe's tennis genius was overshadowed by temper

tantrums, shocking defeats, and a failed marriage to a movie star (Tatum O'Neal). Despite occasional flashes of brilliance, including an outstanding 1984 season, in the wake of Borg's retirement McEnroe found it difficult to focus on his tennis.

In 1990, McEnroe endured the ignominy of being ejected from the Australian Open, becoming the first player since 1963 to be disqualified from a grand slam tournament for misconduct, after one code violation too many in his fourth-round match against Mikael Pernfors.

McEnroe retired from the professional tour at the end of 1992, ending his illustrious singles career ranked 20th in the world.

Without tennis, Borg's world collapsed. Divorce was quickly followed by a second failed marriage, not to mention a child born to another woman, bankruptcy and an alleged overdose of sleeping pills. Borg was attempting, and failing quite catastrophically, to live in a world without tennis.

However, Borg managed to bounce back as the owner of the Björn Borg fashion label, which went on to become extremely successful, second only to Calvin Klein in his home country.

And McEnroe? The man once christened 'Superbrat' by the British media is a genuine celebrity. Gone are the days of the long frizzy hair and the firebrand attitude. Instead, McEnroe's perceptive and amusing opinions see him as one of the most respected commentators and analysts.

Unlike the simmering resentment that existed between the era's other great sporting rivals, Muhammad Ali and Joe Frazier, these two legendary tennis players have only the greatest respect for one another.

Incredibly, Borg and McEnroe met competitively only 14 times between their first encounter in Stockholm in 1978 and the US Open final in 1981. By contrast, Chris Evert and Martina Navratilova met 80 times, Boris Becker and Stefan Edberg 35 times, and Pete Sampras and Andre Agassi 34 times.

Neither man won a major beyond the age of 25. They spent the greater part of their fuel reserves on each other in a fierce rivalry that was informed by respect. McEnroe had too much esteem for Borg ever to go more than, in his own words, "a little nutty" against him. And when he did, in their third encounter in

New Orleans in 1979, Borg simply called McEnroe to the net, put an arm around him, and told him to "just relax". It never happened again.

Borg and McEnroe split their 14 matches seven apiece, and one might have imagined that with Borg's premature retirement the 22-year-old McEnroe would have breathed a sigh of relief and assiduously set about collecting more majors. However, the supremely gifted McEnroe won just three more grand slam titles.

After Borg retired, the lack of competition against the one man against whom he measured himself – in fact, the only tennis player he respected – meant McEnroe was never the same again. Neither was Borg. But the indelible memories that this rivalry has left behind ensures a legacy that no other in the men's game could ever hope to emulate.

Verdict: With seven wins apiece, they can't be separated. McEnroe won three of their four grand slam finals, but Borg's 11 career grand slam victories (with a staggering 41 per cent success rate in the slams he entered) outstrip McEnroe's seven. An honourable draw.

Jack Nicklaus

vs

Arnold Palmer

To perform at their best, great sporting heroes must have great sporting rivals, and they didn't come much bigger and more iconic than the greatest of all golfing rivalries: Arnold Palmer and Jack Nicklaus.

The game of golf has thrown up many fascinating rivalries over the years, from Gene Sarazen and Walter Hagen, Sam Snead and Ben Hogan, to Tiger Woods and Phil Mickelson, not to mention several involving Nicklaus himself. The Golden Bear's tussles with Gary Player, Lee Trevino and, in particular, Tom Watson are the stuff of legend. However, all of these fall short of a rivalry that has shaped the entire history of the game and one that will never be bettered.

Palmer came from a poor background, Nicklaus was privileged; Palmer was made for Hollywood, Nicklaus was a chubby kid with a crew cut; Palmer drew the ball, Nicklaus played with a fade. To call theirs a love-hate relationship would be far too simple, because while both extremes were there, so were many other emotions. Take your pick from admiration, disdain, envy, and a sense of fraternity that could extend to blood-brotherhood.

Arnold Palmer was born in Latrobe, Pennsylvania, on September 10th, 1929. He learned golf from his father, Deacon Palmer, who was the head professional and greenskeeper at Latrobe Country Club. This position allowed a young Arnold to accompany his father as he maintained the course.

He attended Wake Forest University on a golf scholarship, but left after the death of close friend Bud Worsham and enlisted in the United States Coastguard, where he served for three years and had a little time to hone his golf skills. However, Palmer then returned to college and competitive golf, and it was his win in the 1954 US Amateur that made him decide to try the professional tour, and, alongside his new bride, Winifred Walzer, Palmer travelled the circuit in 1955.

Palmer won the 1955 Canadian Open in his rookie season, and raised his game status for several subsequent seasons. His magnetic charisma was a big factor in establishing golf as a television event in the 1950s and 1960s, laying the foundations for the popularity it enjoys today. His first Major championship win at the 1958 Masters established Palmer as one of the leading stars in golf: 'The King' had been crowned.

Palmer is also credited with securing the status of The Open Championship (British Open) among US players. After Ben Hogan won the tournament in 1953, few American professionals had travelled to play in The Open due to its travel requirements, relatively small prize purse, and the style of its links courses (radically different from most American courses).

Palmer was convinced by his business partner, Mark McCormack, that success in The Open – to emulate the feats of Bobby Jones, Walter Hagen, Sam Snead and Hogan before him – would make him a global sporting star, not simply a leading American golfer. So, Palmer travelled to Scotland in 1960, having already won both the Masters and US Open, to try to emulate Hogan's 1953 feat of winning all three in a single year.

He failed, losing out to Kel Nagle by a single shot, but his subsequent Open wins in the early 1960s convinced many American professionals that a trip to Britain would be worth the effort, and it certainly secured Palmer's popularity among British and European fans.

Palmer's most prolific years were 1960 to 1963, when he won 29 PGA Tour events, including five Majors. In 1960, he won the Hickok Belt as the top professional athlete of the year and *Sports Illustrated* magazine's 'Sportsman of the Year' award.

But it was also in 1960 that 20-year-old Jack William Nicklaus announced himself to the golfing world. In between winning two US Amateurs in 1959 and 1961, this young firebrand challenged for the 1960 US Open.

The tournament was held at Cherry Hills Country Club in Englewood, Colorado, and was the scene of the greatest comeback in US Open history by one Arnold Palmer. Cheered on by Arnie's Army, the vocal gallery who followed him in hordes at every major tournament, and who made life hell for his opponents, Palmer erased a seven-stroke deficit during the final round to win his only US Open title.

But Nicklaus was also in contention during the final round, briefly holding the lead. However, two three-putts on the back nine saw him finish two strokes behind Palmer. His second-place finish was the best showing by an amateur since Johnny Goodman won the 1933 US Open.

Nicklaus turned professional toward the end of 1961, and the following year, at the 1962 US Open at Oakmont, he announced himself on the world stage. Played in Palmer's backyard, at Oakmont Country Club, a short putt from his hometown of Latrobe, the Open saw Nicklaus match the local favourite shot for shot.

Nicklaus was threatening to dethrone Palmer and his 'army' didn't like it, taunting him with shouts of "Fat Jack". However, Nicklaus was unfazed. He charged back from five strokes down in the final round to force a play-off with Palmer, which he went on to win, securing him the first of his 18 Majors.

The game's greatest rivalry was born. "Now that the big guy is out of the cage," Palmer said, "everybody better run for cover."

At the age of just 22, Nicklaus was the youngest US Open champion since Bobby Jones (21) in 1923, and he has remained the youngest winner since. Nicklaus played the final 36 holes with Ben Hogan, who later remarked he had just played 36 holes with a kid who should have won by 10 shots.

His rise to fame so soon after turning professional brought him significant endorsement income off the golf course. These business opportunities were facilitated by Mark McCormack, who also managed Palmer and Gary Player, and it was this triumvirate who became known as golf's 'Big Three'.

Golf was growing rapidly in popularity and media coverage increased during the early 1960s, led by the performances of these star players. But Palmer was indisputably the most popular and still the biggest draw for the fans.

In 1963 Nicklaus won two of the four Majors, the Masters and the PGA Championship. These victories made him the then-youngest winner of the Masters and third-youngest winner of the PGA, with each win coming in only his second year as a professional.

In 1964, Palmer won the Masters, but Nicklaus replied by winning the same tournament two years in a row (in 1965 and 1966), becoming the first golfer to achieve such a feat. He also won The Open Championship in 1966, completing his career slam of Major championships at just 26, the youngest man to do so. After a barren haul in 1968 and 1969, Nicklaus then won another Open Championship in 1970.

As the 1960s came to an end, Nicklaus and Player had both acquired clear ascendancy in the game, but Palmer (who won a PGA Tour event every year from 1955 to 1971 inclusive) enjoyed a revival in 1971, winning four events.

But it was Nicklaus whose success rocketed into the stratosphere. Between 1971 and 1980, he would win a further nine Major Championships, overtake Bobby Jones's record of 13 Majors, and become the first player to complete double and triple career slams of golf's four professional Majors.

And then, at the age of 46, and very much in the twilight of his career, came arguably his greatest victory. Nicklaus claimed his 18th and final Major at the 1986 Masters, becoming the championship's oldest winner.

This was The Golden Bear's sixth Masters victory, and it was secured under incredible circumstances when he posted a six-under-par 30 on Augusta's back nine for a final round of 65.

What is also worth bearing in mind when considering Nicklaus's achievements is that during the 25 years when he won his 18 major championships, he also finished second an astounding 18 times (not including his second-place finish at the 1960 US Open as an amateur).

It is sometimes hard for later sporting generations to

understand the achievements and status of former titans. Those who have grown up believing Tiger Woods to be the greatest golfer on the planet may be unaware that his mantle previously belonged to Nicklaus.

However, those who grew up in the Golden Bear's majestic years may not appreciate just how dominant Palmer used to be, both in the eyes of the public and on the course. Only then did Nicklaus appear on the scene to give him his greatest challenge.

It is difficult, too, for a British audience to understand quite how powerfully their rivalry affected the American golfing public.

Nicklaus was always warmly appreciated by British crowds who were thrilled by his skills and taken by the glamour of his appearance. But for many years he was reviled by the Americans as the upstart who dared to challenge their hero.

Palmer excited people, not just for what he was but for what he represented: the true and eternal values of blue-collar America. He was clean-cut and square-jawed; he spoke as straight as he drove a golf ball: a regular guy with a god-given talent.

This is why he inspired such devotion from the thousands who made up Arnie's Army. But while the 'army' drove Jack mad at times, he could also drive Palmer crazy simply by the way he played the game. Nicklaus was, in Palmer's eyes, a gloriously gifted grinder, anathema to a man who would never play a safe shot if there was a spectacular alternative.

The pair's respective gifts were reflected in their later careers when the days of Major wins were behind them. Palmer, the honest, straight-talking straight hitter, pulled in millions as the US's leading celebrity endorser. Nicklaus turned his analytical brain to course design, creating a lucrative worldwide empire.

Palmer and Nicklaus *were* golf for a long time, and to many they still are. From 1958 through 1980, either Palmer or Nicklaus or both enjoyed a top-three finish in at least one Major every year except 1969, a period in which Palmer had 36 top-10s in Grand Slam events, Nicklaus a whopping 59.

Modest in victory, always gracious in defeat, Arnold Palmer and Jack Nicklaus enjoyed a fierce rivalry. But, being a decade older than his biggest rival, Palmer was generous with advice if Nicklaus wanted it, something Nicklaus never forgot even while their spirited competition endured.

Their impact on the game will never be forgotten – it is too far reaching, too indelible. However, when it comes to deciding who came out on top, the greater success of the boy from Ohio sees Nicklaus as the victor.

What made Nicklaus uniquely suited to tournament golf was his mind. In mental application, unrelenting competitiveness and strategic clarity, Nicklaus stands alone. But Palmer's legacy, the way in which he brought the game to the masses, is testimony to what he achieved. Golf will never see their like again.

Verdict: Palmer showcased golf to the people and revolutionised how the game was played, but Nicklaus's monumental success and legacy means he is the outright winner.

The Ashes

While cricket had been played in England since around 1550, it wasn't until 1877 that the Marylebone Cricket Club (MCC) decided to promote the game abroad. Cricket's governing body appointed James Lillywhite to organise a tour to Australia and, after the long voyage, the two sides squared up at the Melbourne Cricket Ground (MCG) on March 15. England were expected to trounce the colony but Australia won the match by 45 runs. Two weeks later England won the rematch and the series was drawn. This largely good-tempered affair turned out to be the exception rather than the norm, as subsequent series featured, according to Harry Pearson: 'Some of the loudest rows, fiercest finger-pointing and most unpleasant facial hair in the history of sport.'

England's 1878-79 tour, led by Lord Harris, was a classic case in point. The hostilities had begun several months earlier when Australia were in England. They were about to play Middlesex at Lord's when the great champion of English cricket, W.G. Grace, turned up to persuade friend and star Australian batsman Billy Midwinter to ditch his country for their county side, Gloucestershire, for a crucial match against Surrey at The Oval. Midwinter agreed and slipped out of the ground with Grace. Three Australian players gave chase and an angry altercation followed. The Australian media was quick to pounce on Grace: 'We in Australia do not take kindly to WG. For such a big man he is surprisingly tenacious on very small points.'

There was only a single Test match during the following tour of Australia, which was again won by the hosts at the MCG. Pace-man Fred Spofforth bowled his side to victory with 13 wickets in the match. Lord Harris was so disappointed that he threw his bat across the pavilion. An unofficial rematch was hastily arranged in Sydney so the tourists could save face, but the atmosphere was tense, the crowd restless.

When umpire George Coulthard gave local boy Billy Murdoch his marching orders, two thousand spectators streamed onto the pitch to confront the English players, forcing several to defend themselves with stumps. As a result, when the Australians toured England the following year many clubs refused to play them. The tone had been set for the series that gave birth to the legend of the Ashes.

The sides had each won a series before England hosted the Australians on their 1882 tour. In the only Test match at The Oval, Australia posted 63 in their first innings. England also batted poorly however and could only manage 101. It was destined to be a low-scoring affair when Australia limped to 122 in their second innings, setting England just 85 for victory. They might have been defending a bigger lead had it not been for a little gamesmanship, or what we'd now call sledging, from a noted master of the art: Grace.

Sam Jones played the ball to the doctor but decided against running. Grace then beckoned him over. Jones saw nothing untoward in the gesture and approached the great man. As soon as he was out of his crease, Grace threw down the stumps and appealed for the run out. Fred Spofforth was so incensed by the umpire's decision to give Jones out that he vowed revenge. The following day he tore through England's batting line-up and posted figures of 7-44. However, England only needed 10 runs for victory when their last batsman, Ted Peate, came to the crease. He only managed to get two before being bowled by Harry Boyle.

England went into shock. And four days later Reginald Brooks penned the immortal mock obituary for English cricket in the *Sporting Times*:

In Affectionate Remembrance
of
ENGLISH CRICKET,
which died at the Oval
on
29th AUGUST, 1882,
Deeply lamented by a large circle of sorrowing
friends and acquaintances.
R.I.P.
N.B.—The body will be cremated and the
ashes taken to Australia.

Although the obituary did not appear in the Australian media, they quickly adopted the term when England's captain for the 1882-83 tour, Ivo Bligh, repeatedly mentioned returning home with the ashes during the build-up to the Test series. Indeed, it was while on this tour that Bligh was presented with the famous urn.

There are several versions of this story but only two seem credible: Bligh claimed Florence Morphy, who would later become his wife and who was a member of a Victorian Ladies' club, had given him the urn after the third Test. However, recent research suggests that Sir William Clarke may have presented the piece to Bligh, who was now Lord Darnley, after a private match on his estate earlier in the tour. Even the contents of the tiny urn have provoked heated debate, although it is now widely accepted that the ashes are the remains of a single bail.

The word 'ashes' fell out of common usage for the next twenty years and was only resurrected when Australian George Giffen penned his memoirs, *With Bat & Ball*, in 1899, in which he often used it. And Pelham Warner vowed to regain 'the ashes' for England in 1903. Having done so, he published *How We Recovered The Ashes*, thus cementing the status of the contest.

The urn, however, was not presented to the winning team. In fact it was not until it was donated to the MCC by Darnley's widow after his death in 1927 that the urn entered the public domain. Before then the Ashes had simply been an intangible concept: now they had a physical embodiment. Today it is believed that the urn is an official cricket trophy but it is in fact a private memento, which is why the fragile original museum piece is never awarded to the winning team.

England dominated towards the end of the 19th century, with the 1894-95 tour making most of the headlines. Australia posted a huge total in the first Test in Sydney and then dismissed the visitors for 325. Enforcing the follow-on, they then restricted England to 437 in their second innings. Needing just 177 for victory, Australia cruised to 133 for 2 by the close of play on the penultimate day. Heavy overnight rain made the pitch unplayable the following morning, however, and Bobby Peel's 6-67 gave England victory by just ten runs. England won the deciding Test and took the series 3-2. Under the captaincy of W.G. Grace, they also won the home 1896 series.

The matches may have been closely fought but bitterness lingered over the professional element that was creeping into the English game. If Grace was playing, many grounds would increase their admission fees, and it was an ill-kept secret that even as an amateur he was being paid to play. Indeed, he is said to have received £3000 (around £100,000 today) to tour Australia in 1891-92, while the rest of the team usually only received expenses.

This was an issue that had been bubbling away for some time. During the 1884-85 series the Australian team refused to play in the Melbourne Test unless they were offered half the gate receipts. Their demands were viewed as unacceptable and eleven new players were selected. Then, Englishman Billy Barnes tried to punch Australian captain Percy McDonnell while the two were arguing over players' pay, and he ended up breaking his hand on a wall. The tourists also vented their frustration at the umpires. George Hodges was so distressed by the abuse that he refused to take the field in the final Test.

The two sides were evenly matched in the lead-up to the First World War and they shared a number of surprisingly good-tempered series. This was to change in the 1920s. Under their ruthless but brilliant captain, Warwick Armstrong, Australia only lost once to England in 15 Tests between the end of the war and 1925. They pioneered the tactic of using two fast bowlers, Ted McDonald and Jack Gregory, in tandem to apply pressure on the hapless English.

England enjoyed an upturn in fortune towards the end of the decade, thanks largely to the superb batting of Wally Hammond, Jack Hobbs and Herbert Sutcliffe, and they won the 1928-29 series comfortably. But by the following series, the tide had turned once more. Australian Donald Bradman had looked promising on home soil, but in 1930 he totally dominated the English bowlers in conditions they were used to. He scored 974 runs at an average of 139.14, a world record for a single series that has stood for more than 80 years. Bradman's peerless batting, ably supported by Bill Woodfull and Bill Ponsford, posed such a threat that to have any chance of beating Australia

England would need to figure out a way to negate them. Faced with such a fearsome batting line-up England's Douglas Jardine developed a bowling tactic that would lead to the most controversial series in cricket history: Bodyline.

England had learned from their 1925 defeat and were blessed with two lethal fast bowlers, Harold Larwood and Bill Voce. Jardine instructed them to bowl short-pitched deliveries on the line of the body so that the unprotected Australian batsmen would have to fend the balls off towards a stacked leg-side field.

Having been struck a fearful blow in the chest, Australian captain Bill Woodfull collapsed. When England manager Pelham Warner went to their changing rooms at the end of the day's play to see if he was all right, Woodfull was none too pleased at the way the game was being played: "There are two teams out there. One of them is trying to play cricket, the other is making no attempt to do so."

Some of Woodfull's team-mates suggested they employ the same leg-theory bowling, but Woodfull, to his credit, was having none of it. Jardine refused to buckle to the pressure from the media and crowds at each game, however, and continued urging his bowlers to aim at the Australian batsmen, particularly Bradman. But when Bert Oldfield was taken off with a fractured skull, the Australian Cricket Board knew it had to intervene. It sent this telegram to the MCC:

'Bodyline bowling is causing intensely bitter feelings between our players, as well as injury. In our opinion it is unsportsmanlike and, unless stopped at once, it is likely to upset the friendly relations between England and Australia.'

The English ignored the message and took the series 4-1, but the Australian protests weren't ignored for long and the MCC eventually changed the laws of the game to limit the number of leg-side fielders. Indeed, the MCC blamed Larwood for inflaming the international incident and banned him from playing in the 1934 series unless he apologised, which he refused to do. Without their other star bowler, Voce, or Jardine, England were no match for Woodfull's Australians, a trend that continued when Bradman took over the captaincy in 1936.

The incomparable batsman was still at the helm when the

series resumed after the Second World War, but his own form had slumped and he was thinking of retiring. In the first Test at Brisbane he made an unconvincing start and was only on 28 when he edged the ball to Jack Ikin at second slip. England claimed the catch but Bradman refused to walk. The umpire agreed with him that it was a bump ball and Bradman went on to make a magnificent 187. Sadly for England, this crucial and much-debated incident ushered in Bradman's Indian summer.

On their 1948 tour of England, the Australians played 34 matches. They won 27 and drew seven and, as a result, were lauded as the 'Invincibles'. Aside from remaining unbeaten, the tour will be remembered for Bradman's last Test innings. He only needed four runs in The Oval Test to end his career with an average of exactly 100 but he didn't pick a googly from Eric Hollies and made a second-ball duck.

Although England were denied the Ashes until 1953, they then enjoyed a brief resurgence. The Australian batsmen couldn't cope with the pace of Frank Tyson and Brian Statham, or the spin of Jim Laker, who came away from the 1956 Old Trafford Test with the remarkable bowling figures of 19 for 90. There hadn't been much controversy in the decade but that was about to change.

On the 1958-59 tour to Australia the England team were concerned about Ian Meckiff's bowling action. England's captain, Peter May, claimed the Australian was throwing the ball with a bent elbow, not bowling it with a straight arm. The Australian camp countered that his arm had small degree of permanent flex due to a genetic abnormality, and he helped his side to a comfortable series win. The furore wouldn't subside, however, and Meckiff's career was eventually ended when he was repeatedly called for 'chucking' in the 1963 series against South Africa.

The 1960s were dull by comparison. Under the captaincy of first Bob Simpson and then Bill Lawry, the Australians were prepared to eke out boring draws so they could retain the Ashes. The media were quick to condemn the slow-play tactics because spectator numbers were falling alarmingly, but the players refused to back down. A lively series was needed to put cricket back on the sporting map… And that's just what it got.

When Ray Illingworth led the 1970-71 tourists to Australia they hadn't held the Ashes for fifteen years. They arrived with hostile intent and with sledging entering its first golden age there was extra spice between the combatants. England's John Snow was quite prepared to bounce the Australian tail-enders, but things soon spiralled out of control when he hit Terry Jenner on the head. As Snow made his way to the boundary at the end of the over, fans on the notorious Sydney Hill pelted him with beer cans. He was then confronted by an angry spectator screaming 'Bodyline!'

Having tried but failed to calm things down, Illingworth had no option but to lead his team from the field. They only reappeared when the referee warned them that they were about to forfeit the match. England won the series 2-0 and reignited interest in the Ashes in both countries.

Master sledgers and fearsome bowlers Jeff Thomson and Dennis Lillee dominated the English batsmen throughout the 1970s with their pace and bounce, but it was with the bat, at the WACA in 1979, that Lillee had his most controversial moment. He marched out to the middle with an aluminium blade and, every time he hit the ball, the noise echoed around the ground. The English players complained that it was damaging the ball and the umpires upheld the complaint. Lillee, of course, wouldn't go quietly and hurled the bat across the outfield.

Under the shrewd captaincy of Mike Brearley, England turned the tables and enjoyed a decade of success in the 1980s. However, affairs had begun in miserable fashion for the home side during the Australian tour of England in 1981 when Ian Botham was stripped of the captaincy after a run of poor results. His side were 1-0 down going into the third Test at Headingley, but with Brearley back at the helm, and with the shackles seemingly removed, Botham suddenly seemed inspired.

Looking down and out after being asked to follow on, and struggling at 135-7 in their second innings, Botham smashed 149 not out and gave England a lead of 130. Bob Willis then steamed in and bowled England to the unlikeliest of victories with figures of 8-43. Although Botham produced several memorable performances during the series, his heroics at Headingley left a lasting impression on the Australian players, particularly a

31

young Allan Border.

When Border took over the captaincy, he decided that the 'having a beer with the opposition at the end of the day' approach was past its sell-by date. He was determined to captain a mentally and physically tough side that would never take a backward step, either with bat or ball, or in the sledging stakes. Under Mark Taylor and Steve Waugh, players like Shane Warne, Merv Hughes and Glenn McGrath carried on this tradition and Australia dominated the series for eighteen years.

This team was particularly tough to beat because they held a psychological edge over the English. In Hughes they had the finest sledger of his generation, in Warne perhaps the greatest leg spinner of all time, and McGrath, himself no slouch in the sledging stakes, was the most accurate fast bowler. Ricky Ponting inherited much of the side when he took over the captaincy in 2004 but, despite dispatching most of the other Test playing nations, England were to prove much sterner opposition by the time they toured in 2005.

This didn't stop Glenn McGrath winding the English up with his customary pre-series prediction: "We'll win 5-0. I'd be letting myself and my team-mates down if I said anything else."

This only seemed to unite the English bowlers and they came out firing in the first Test at Lord's. Steve Harmison battered Justin Langer with a series of ferocious deliveries, then hit Matthew Hayden on the head. He followed this up by striking Ponting on the helmet, the blow forcing his protective grille into his face and drawing blood. The crowd absolutely loved it and were baying for more.

Langer marched over to England's Andrew Strauss to ask why no one was checking on Ponting and said: "This really is a war out here, isn't it?"

Strauss and the remaining English players didn't say a word. They went on to lose the Test but they had shown that they would be no pushover. Indeed they fought back magnificently to take arguably the best series of all time 2-1, with last gasp victories at Edgbaston and Trent Bridge.

Dennis Lillee summed up the thoughts of a nation with: "Losing to other sides is not the end of the world, but losing the Ashes is."

Australia recovered quickly and, with McGrath and Warne on the verge of retirement, they thumped England on the 2006-07 tour, posting a 5-0 series whitewash. With Australia losing several of their best players, the 2009 tour to England promised to be a tense encounter. Justin Langer even produced a dossier on how to sledge the English players and how the Australians should cope with the feral atmosphere at some of the grounds.

After a hard-fought draw in Cardiff, England won at Lord's for the first time in 75 years. However, Australia rallied and took the Headingley Test by an innings. The stage was set for the deciding Test at the Oval and England did not disappoint, winning the match and with it the series, 2-1. They then headed down under for what was predicted to be a tight 2010-11 Ashes battle. But by now Australia were a team in decline. England won comfortably, their first series win in Australia for 24 years, with three of their victories by innings margins.

Sixty-six series have been played since 1882. Australia lead 31-30, with five having been drawn (in which case the side holding the Ashes automatically retains them). Overall, Australia have won 123 matches to England's 100, with 87 games ending in draws.

The epic 2005 series, like the celebrated 1981 encounter, repeatedly brought England to a standstill during the summer as the combatants played out incredible matches with nail-biting conclusions. This popularity used to be the preserve of the major sports like football but, with each success, the game grows in popularity in the competing countries. The Ashes, it seems, are here to stay.

Verdict: Australia surprised the mother country when the series began but England soon recovered. The Bradman era saw Australia ease clear, and they maintained that dominance for much of the latter half of the 20th century. The new millennium has seen England grow in confidence and, since 2005, they have been the dominant force. Recent form, however, cannot hide the overall statistics and Australia take the contest on points.

The Fantastic Four: Leonard, Hearns, Hagler & Duran

When it comes to the greatest sporting rivalries, the contests generally fall into two specific categories: two individuals or two teams. However, there is one major exception to this rule, and it comes from a sport that is, in many ways, defined by its rivalries.

In the late 1970s, boxing was in a state of decline and the heavyweight division's self-styled 'Greatest' champion, Muhammad Ali, had just decided to retire after an imperious career. But the sport was to spark dramatically back to life thanks to an unbelievable series of fights that involved four completely dissimilar men, who would all eventually fight as middleweights: Sugar Ray Leonard, Roberto Duran, Marvin Hagler and Thomas Hearns.

Of the four, Sugar Ray Leonard was arguably the fans' favourite. The man with the lightning-fast fists and well-defined moves had been loved by the nation ever since he flashed his supreme skills and captivating personality at the 1976 Montreal Olympics en route to a welterweight gold medal. He was telegenic and articulate, with a mega-watt smile that exuded charisma.

But when he returned from the Games, a professional career was the last thing Leonard wanted. He had planned to retire and accept a scholarship to the University of Maryland, but a paternity suit that came without warning saw his promised endorsements evaporate. And so if he was to capitalise on his Olympic success it meant he would have to embark on a career in the one profession he knew best.

Roberto Duran, meanwhile, had begun his career as a featherweight, and had garnered a reputation almost as fearsome as his arrogant nature. Duran had rocketed through the international rankings and won his first world title when he beat Scotland's tartan-shorted Ken Buchanan for the WBA lightweight title in June 1972 in New York.

The owner of the fully deserved nickname 'Manos de Piedra' (Hands of Stone), Duran was a man blessed with an insatiable desire to destroy all those who had the gall to challenge him and the devastating punch to seal the deal. However, he also boasted supreme defensive skills with which to control his opponent. These skills matched with his bravery and unrelenting aggression made him one of the all-time great boxers and a man to be feared.

Duran was also known for his machismo and a swagger that bordered on bullying, and he simply didn't care about getting under the skin of his opponents; in fact, he revelled in it. He was to dominate the lightweight scene for almost a decade, unifying the titles and amassing an incredible record of 71 wins and just one defeat.

He then decided to move up to welterweight to take on the boxer he saw as his nemesis, the reigning WBC welterweight champion Sugar Ray Leonard, a man he would go on to fight in three significant bouts.

But it was the first two fights in the legendary Leonard-Duran trilogy that would usher in this last great era of boxing, the first of which took place on June 20th, 1980, on the very stage where he had won the Olympic final against Cuba's Andrés Aldama four years earlier.

This first fight would be affectionately known as the 'Brawl in Montreal', and it was, from almost the opening salvo, a fight that belonged to Duran. Each round seemed to descend into an intense three-minute slugfest. Duran was landing body shot after body shot that would have felled lesser fighters and Leonard was struggling.

But the reigning champion finally sprang into life in the fifth round, unleashing dazzling combinations. Duran countered the best way he knew, rough-housing Leonard, even using his head as a weapon whenever Leonard tried to come inside.

However, it wasn't just the brute force of Duran's street-fighting style that would see Leonard lose for the first time in his professional career; it was his foolish mistake in taking on the Panamanian at his own game. Leonard's legendary trainer, Angelo Dundee, had counselled Leonard to box, to move side to side and not to get caught on the ropes, but Leonard decided to fight Duran's way. "Flat-footed," he said. "I will not run."

As the rounds went into double figures Leonard rallied further, throwing everything he had at Duran. When the final bell sounded, Leonard reached out and tried to tap Duran with his glove, but the little man ignored the gesture and went to his corner to await the verdict.

For a brief moment it appeared that this desperately close fight may even be declared a draw but the final judge's decision rendered the result a majority verdict. Clearly disappointed, Sugar Ray didn't query the decision. Duran was the deserved victor, a man who had just vanquished a fighter who was quicker and more skilled than he was by sheer will. It was an unbelievable performance.

Leonard, not one for hiding his light under a bushel, had also been out-swaggered. His opponent exuded confidence, while Leonard, even before the fight, had worn the look of a man who already knew his fate.

At first Sugar Ray thought about packing it all in, but after a while he couldn't stem the tide of revenge that was building inside him. Courtesy of the erstwhile promoter Don King, who held the promotional rights to Duran-Leonard II, the rematch was scheduled for November 25th, 1980 and would take place in New Orleans's Louisiana Superdome.

If Duran had won the first fight through his indomitable willpower, that same spirit was completely obliterated in the rematch, although this fight would never be regarded as being a bout worthy of the highest plaudits. However, on a barmy New Orleans night, what happened transcended not just boxing but any sport.

This time Leonard was in peak condition, both physically and mentally. Duran, on the other hand, had not prepared well. His poor diet and love of partying had not helped matters. By the seventh round, Duran's attempts to end the fight destructively were being exposed as humiliatingly futile. As his frustration grew, the baring of teeth that had suggested the Panamanian's familiar sneer began to convey a sickly embarrassment.

When the bell rang for the seventh round, Leonard began taunting as elaborately contemptuous as anything Muhammad Ali ever pulled. He stuck his chin out to invite punches and turned his back-side towards his victim, once winding up his right hand ludicrously as if to throw a bolo punch, before launching his left at Duran's chin.

Many watching thought these antics would enrage Duran and provoke him to a level of savagery that skirted the rules of the sport. However, butting and kicking would have been infinitely less surprising than what he did.

With seconds remaining in the eighth round, Duran quit, first telling referee Octavio Meyran: "I do not want to fight this clown," before uttering the immortal words that are now synonymous with the fight, "No mas".

Duran's fierce brilliance and macho disdain persuaded practically all who saw him that he was a fighting man to his bones, and so his decision to quit was as bizarre as anything the most experienced watchers at ringside had ever seen.

The bravest man in the sport had committed boxing's greatest sin, and even today he is at a loss to explain why. At the time he cited severe stomach cramps, which, given the Panamanian's infamous diet, may have had some basis. Plus, the Baptist Hospital in New Orleans did accept, after an examination in the early hours of Wednesday morning, that there had been acute abdominal pains.

But during the 20-odd minutes of action against Leonard there was no sign of agony and nothing less could have been expected to undermine the will of Roberto Duran. It was perhaps the most famous act of surrender in ring history, but no-one, even today, doubts Duran's bravery inside the ropes.

Most agree that his quitting was most likely caused by frustration rather than a lack of courage. Some think that Duran believed he was committing the ultimate macho act, while Leonard is in no doubt that he quit out of humiliation, like "one of those things that happens to bullies".

Unfortunately, Duran's surrender all but overshadowed Leonard's superb performance. However, as Ray admitted: "I made him quit – and making Roberto Duran quit was even better than knocking him out. The fact that he quit and the way he did it doesn't take anything away from my victory. I'm the champion because he couldn't change and I could."

Despite these two monumental fights, it is perhaps the two fights between Hearns and Leonard that saw the most fascinating rivalry between the four emerge. Their first fight in 1981 was billed as 'The Showdown' for the unified welterweight championship and it was one of the most eagerly anticipated bouts not just in the welterweight division but in boxing history.

The 'Hit Man' was an intimidating presence and unquestionably one of the greatest fighters of his (or any) era. The first boxer to win world titles in four different weight categories, he went on to claim eight belts in six weight divisions.

Hearns – the proud owner of a 78-inch wingspan – had the innate ability to control a fight with his long jab (considered to be one of the best – if not *the* best – in the business), before ending proceedings instantly with his sledgehammer right.

He won 61 fights in his career (48 by knockout) and claimed the likes of Wilfred Benitez and Pipino Cuevas amongst his scalps. But it was his fights against Duran and Hagler, and his two epic bouts against Leonard that cemented his place at boxing's top table.

The duel that defined both Leonard and Hearns was the first of their two iconic bouts on September 16th, 1981: a contest that fulfilled its breathless billing and took place in boxing's very own Asgaard, Las Vegas.

Going into the fight Leonard was WBC welterweight champion, while Hearns was the reigning WBA holder. What was to transpire was a fight that boasted more ebbs and flows than anything the best Hollywood scriptwriter could have dreamed up.

In the sixth round, Leonard rocked the Hit Man with a powerful left hook but Hearns immediately adapted his tactics and reverted to the style that he'd used to clinical effect in his amateur days, sticking his rapier-like left jab in Leonard's face and piling on the points.

By the 13th round Hearns was ahead on points and, with his left eye closing under the bombardment, and his reputation on the line, Leonard heard Angelo Dundee tell him in the same harsh voice that had so galvanised Muhammad Ali: "You're blowing it, son."

It was just the jolt that Leonard needed and he responded with blistering effect, staggering Hearns in the next round and then stopping him in the 14th. Under today's 12-round limit Hearns would have reigned supreme, but these were the days of 15-round bouts and Leonard was on top of the world.

The next fight between the four saw Roberto Duran step into the ring to try to become the world middleweight champion against the holder, Marvin Hagler, on November 10th, 1983, with the contest once again taking place in Las Vegas.

'Marvelous' Marvin Hagler was one of the toughest fighters the sport has seen. Originally known simply as Marvin Hagler, the New Jersey native was a man whose hubris often threatened to overshadow his fighting ability.

In the middle of his career, aggrieved that he was not receiving due credit, he decided to change his name to something he considered more apt. He saw himself as awe-inspiring and the soubriquet 'Marvelous' was born, which was soon legally registered just in case anyone dared not refer to him by his correct title.

He was only knocked down once in his 67 career fights, and even then that was considered a 'pushdown', with John Mugabi cuffing him to the canvas.

Hagler's bout against Duran was another all-out war, where there was no chance of either man laying down his arms and calling it quits. It was ferociously competitive and went the full 15 rounds, although after 12 rounds two of the judges had Duran ahead on points.

Hagler, calling on all of his indomitable spirit, fought tenaciously over the final three rounds to earn a unanimous decision. Despite the loss, Duran became the only man ever to last 15 rounds against the great middleweight champion.

Duran wouldn't have to wait long to climb back into the ring as a fight against Hearns was scheduled for June 25th, 1984. Just one month prior to the fight, Sugar Ray Leonard had returned from his self-imposed retirement to fight Kevin Howard in Worcester, Massachusetts.

Howard had knocked Leonard flat on his back in the fourth round, the first knockdown of Leonard's professional career, but Leonard came back to stop Howard in the ninth. However, the stoppage was disputed, with some feeling that the referee stepped in too early, even though Leonard was ahead on all three scorecards at the time.

At the post-fight press conference, Leonard surprised everyone by announcing his second retirement. Suffering from a detached retina in his right eye, and a belief that he simply didn't have what it took any longer, Leonard walked away from boxing.

With Leonard no longer around, the fight between Hearns and Duran took on added significance. The Panamanian was in full macho mode, dismissing Hearns for his performance against Leonard and calling him a chicken. This indifference led to Duran once more embarking on a less than stellar training programme and from the opening seconds of the fight his lack of preparation was glaringly obvious.

Hearns began explosively and floored Duran in the closing minutes of the first round. Then, in the second, he exploded a monstrous right on Duran's jaw, before dropping another flush on his nose. Duran fell to the canvas, out stone cold. It was the only time he was counted out in his career.

His machismo was obliterated, but Hearns refused to put the dagger in, his respect for Duran too great. "I was fighting a legend," Hearns said that night. "Roberto Duran is probably the greatest fighter I've ever been in the ring with."

Hearns's reputation was restored. The Hit Man was back and he was ready to pit his wits against the man who had found it much harder to defeat Duran, 'Marvelous Marvin'. Hagler was the defending middleweight champion and had not lost a fight in nine years, while Hearns, since losing to Leonard four years previously, had won eight fights.

And so on April 15th, 1985, the two men faced off at the appropriately named Caesars Palace. Like two imperious Roman emperors the men entered the ring with one thing on their minds: war.

Most pundits were predicting that a knockout would decide the fight and with an incredible record of 34 KOs from 41 fights, Hearns was fancied.

But they had not reckoned on Hagler's fortitude. By the end of the furious opening round, Hearns was already a spent force. He would later admit, "The first round took everything out of me." Hearns managed to negotiate the second round but, by the third, Hagler began raining barrages down on his opponent, culminating in two massive rights, the second of which dropped Hearns to the canvas.

The war had been fought at a breakneck pace and everyone who was there was sure that they'd witnessed the most action-packed bout they would ever see. Even today, the fight is seen as the zenith of boxing in the latter half of the 20th century, acclaimed by many as the greatest short fight in history.

As for the victor, the devastating nature of his win finally brought Hagler the acclaim he so desperately sought, including the coveted accolade of Fighter of the Year for 1985.

Two years went by without any of the quartet squaring up to one another, but when the next fight was announced it was not the match-up that most people expected: Sugar Ray Leonard had returned.

The much-anticipated fight against the undefeated Hagler generated plenty of controversy because of Leonard's three-year hiatus and his serious eye injuries, yet it also excited sports fans who had hoped to see them fight years earlier.

One thing was certain: Hagler was the overwhelming favourite to retain his world middleweight title, and the man himself was more confident of victory than he had been for any of his previous 12 defences. He was also certain that this fight would confirm his greatness.

Leonard's insistence on the new-fangled championship distance of 12 rounds – instead of 15 – convinced Hagler that the challenger would be short on stamina. But what Hagler couldn't know was that Leonard had spent the last year preparing for the bout with full-on fights behind closed doors, complete with referee, time-keeper, 10-ounce gloves and no headguards, as well as orthodox sparring sessions.

There had been much discussion about the contrast in styles: Hagler was the big-hitting counter-puncher, while Leonard was the quick and elusive showman with his flashy combinations. Who would win, Hagler the self-pronounced bull or Leonard the matador?

Leonard had a strategy that made maximum use of his blink-and-you'll-miss-it punching style. He would hit Hagler in the last 15 seconds of every round with an insanely quick onslaught to try to steal the stanza. This, coupled with his intense preparation, saw him win the first two rounds easily.

Hagler, teased and tormented into becoming the aggressor, was often caught on the way in, yet he still connected with some damaging punches that rocked Leonard, notably in the fifth and ninth.

Leonard, who had planned to attack in hope of exploiting Hagler's occasional vulnerability to cuts, adapted like the natural entertainer he was, dancing out of trouble and often clipping the champion as he slipped out of range.

At the bell, Hagler raised his arms in triumph. Leonard, fatigued by all his ring movement, initially sank to the canvas but then stood to claim victory. The wait for the result seemed to take an eternity, but when it finally came Marvin Hagler's championship reign was over: Leonard had won by a split decision.

The decision was controversial and more than two decades later the debate has barely abated. Hagler still refuses to speak to Leonard.

Many felt that Leonard deserved the decision, arguing that he'd landed more punches, showed better defence and marshalled the ring with far greater authority and skill. Other experts argue that it was Hagler's over-confidence that was his undoing; he was so dismissive of the threat Leonard carried that he let the fight slip away.

Jim Murray, long-time sports columnist for the *Los Angeles Times*, wrote: 'It wasn't even close. He didn't just outpoint Hagler, he exposed him. He made him look like a guy chasing a bus… In snowshoes.'

On June 12th, 1989 Leonard and Hearns, eight years after their first classic fight, fought for the second time. Leonard was the holder of the WBC super-middleweight championship and the defence of his crown more than lived up to its billing as 'The War'.

Hearns dominated early proceedings, knocking Leonard down twice, but Leonard clawed his way back, slowly accumulating points. However, as the fight entered the final round, Leonard needed a knockout to win, and so he set about pulverising Hearns with blow after blow. He scored a rare 10-8 round without a knockdown on one judge's scorecard to earn an incredible draw.

Leonard would later admit that "Tommy won the fight" but, if anything, their second head-to-head proved that they were more evenly matched than ever. A third fight against the Hit Man or another against Hagler may have seemed like a more obvious, not to mention lucrative, option for Leonard, but he had his sights on another opponent.

On December 7th, 1989 on a cold winter's night in Nevada, Leonard would go on to defend his title against Roberto Duran in the ninth and final fight between this fabulous foursome. Unfortunately, this fight was comfortably the least entertaining of their personal trilogy.

Leonard danced and teased Duran, outmanoeuvring him at every turn. He was determined not to let Duran get close enough to inflict any damage, and while his tactics ensured that this would guarantee him victory, it meant that the fight was dull by comparison with their earlier meetings.

As the fight reached its denouement, this time it was the crowd who seemed to be saying "No mas". At the final bell they booed both fighters for the lack of drama, as they knew that Leonard had won comprehensively before the verdict was announced. One statistic had Duran throwing 588 punches but only landing 84.

Looking back with the knowledge that it was the quartet's final match-up, the fight feels like something of an anti-climax. But when you compare it with the majestic encounters that had come before, it was always destined to be second best.

Between them, these four incredible fighters won 16 recognised world titles. To put their achievements in even greater context, when Leonard and Duran fought for the third and final time in 1989, their aggregate record was 229 wins, 15 losses and four draws…and eight of those losses came at the hands of one another.

Boxing's heavyweight division has long been lauded as the sport's Blue Riband category, the one that steals the lustre and loves to bask in its glow. However, it was the memorable fights between these men that gave the glory to the welter-, middle- and super-middleweight divisions.

The quartet brought out the best in each other, their names forever linked as icons from a golden age. Their nine unforgettable bouts spread over one unforgettable decade rewrote the sport's history and helped to provide a legacy that will never be matched.

Verdict: courtesy of both the best career record and the best record in their bouts against each other (four wins, one draw and one loss) the winner is Sugar Ray Leonard. By the time he retired he had won world championships in five different weight classes and his ability to out-think and out-box any opponent set Leonard apart from all but three of his peers.

However, it was his never-say-die attitude that lifted him above these three giants. As the greatest of them all, Muhammad Ali, once said: "To be legendary, you have got to have heart, and Ray's heart was bigger than all the rest," and that is all you need know.

June 20th, 1980	Duran (winner) v Leonard	UD 15	Montreal
November 25th, 1980	Leonard (winner) v Duran	TKO 8	New Orleans
September 16th, 1981	Leonard (winner) v Hearns	TKO 14	Las Vegas
November 10th, 1983	Hagler (winner) v Duran	UD 15	LV
June 15th, 1984	Hearns (winner) v Duran	TKO 2	LV
April 15th, 1985	Hagler (winner) v Hearns	TKO 3	LV
April 6th, 1987	Leonard (winner) v Hagler	SD 12	LV
June 12th, 1989	Hearns/Leonard (draw)	D 12	LV
December 7th, 1989	Leonard (winner) v Duran	UD 12	LV

Sebastian Coe

vs

Steve Ovett

Although the two men only met in seven major competitive races – which seems scarcely believable given that they dominated middle-distance running for a generation – the rivalry between Coe and Ovett is forever imprinted on the consciousness of British and world sport. It was a rivalry that was as much about trading world records as it was trying to better the other on the track. Indeed, it is said that they often deliberately avoided each other to compete at separate events so that they could better the other's time without the distraction of a personal head-to-head.

Steve Ovett was born in Brighton in October 1955. He initially showed great promise as a footballer but grew tired of the inadequacies of less gifted team-mates and opted for a solo career in athletics instead. Many believe that his apparent arrogance and aloofness, which evolved into an unwillingness to give even the best media correspondents much of his time, probably stems from his self-absorption and his own personal desire to succeed. Coe would soon become the fly in the ointment by frequently upstaging Ovett, endearing himself to the press in the process and further highlighting the rivalry.

Ovett's range was extraordinary: when only 15 he ran a sub-50-second 400 metres to win the English Youths title; two years later he ran a four-minute mile; he then won the Under 20 National Cross-Country Championships over a 10-kilometre course by more than a minute; and in 1976 he won a half-marathon in a borrowed pair of shoes in just 65 minutes. His talents weren't confined to the running events either. He set Sussex Junior records in both the high jump and long jump, the latter lasting nearly 20 years. Coach Barry Tilbury took one look at the youngster and said this, a classic case of understatement: "I can't tell you exactly how good he'll be but I think he might make it to the Olympics."

While Ovett was mulling over whether to concentrate on the 400 metres, at which he had the endurance but not quite the power, he ran in several 800-metre events. His first career title came in the European Junior 800 metres in 1973, which he backed up with a silver medal at the following year's senior event in Rome. The shorter of the two middle-distance events was now clearly his preference because he then took silver at the 1974 European Championships (in a junior record time of 1.45.77) and won AAA titles at home for the next three years.

He was selected for the Great Britain team at the Montreal Olympics and proved his worth by making the final, although he only finished fifth after miscalculating his pace over the first lap. He also ran in the 1500 metres but was obstructed in the semi-final and missed out on a medal. These relatively low-key performances were soon overshadowed by his incredible last 200 metres at the inaugural athletics World Cup in 1977, when he left a class field that included Olympic 1500-metre champion John Walker for dead.

Ovett's style had now matured to the point where he would casually track the world's best runners before obliterating them with his ferocious kick. His trademark wave to the crowd as he breezed into the lead down the home straight made him popular with the fans, but the cockiness did not sit well with his contemporaries. Ovett was good enough to back himself, however, and he didn't care much for the opinions of others. He also, initially at least, didn't seem interested in records and was more concerned with winning each race with a flourish rather than watching the clock.

"I don't get caught up in times and never run against the clock. I run against men on the day." Steve Ovett

"He (Ovett) *really is a wonderful athlete but he should not belittle inferior opponents. That is sheer bad manners."* Peter Coe

Sebastian Coe was born in Chiswick, West London, in September 1956 but, having spent a few years in Stratford – where he showed promise as a sprinter and jumper (he wasn't in Ovett's class, however) – he was brought up in Sheffield. He joined the Hallamshire Harriers athletics team at the age of 12 and quickly established himself as a promising middle-distance runner. This raw talent combined with an obsessive will to win was only threatened by his desire to improve upon his own times. Losing was never an option, be it at cricket on the beach, tennis against his parents or racing to the shops and back.

His father, Peter, continued to train him but Coe Senior was a hard taskmaster. Schoolboy athlete Kim McDonald recalled seeing the young Sebastian in tears after being scolded whenever he ran poorly. But, despite the harsh words, Peter finally recognised that he was dealing with someone who had immense talent. That talent now needed to be nurtured and exploited to get the most out of an extraordinary athlete.

His first few cross-country races as a schoolboy didn't go to plan, and it was only in 1971 that Coe was noticed, when he won a mile race against much older opposition. Peter now firmly believed his son would go to the 1980 Olympics and that became the pair's goal. Coe lived and breathed it throughout his junior career but this wouldn't be enough unless he put in the hard ten-mile training runs in the depths of an English winter. He also trained hard on his speed and was soon delivering sub-22-second 200-metre times.

He then went to Loughborough University, where Peter continued to train him – albeit alongside visionary coach George Gandy – by devising strict speed endurance training routines and set patterns for the various stages of each race. Coe was also developing a distinctive running style, but it was markedly different from Ovett's. Where the Brighton man was happy to sit back and wait for the right moment to strike, the more languid Coe liked to dominate from the gun. His blistering first-lap pace usually weeded out the also-rans (and often did for the best runners, too), but he sometimes came unstuck himself and was often found wanting for pace when it mattered most: in the last 200 metres. Coe refined his strategy however, and he was eventually able to combine raw speed with natural endurance. Indeed, he was soon so good that pacemakers had to be enlisted so he could defeat his greatest enemy: the clock.

Although the pair had met at an English Schools cross-country race in 1972 (Ovett came second, Coe tenth), had Coe pursued his dream of becoming a 5000-metre runner that might have been it and the sporting world would have been denied one of its greatest rivalries. As it is, the stage was now set for more than a decade of gripping tussles between the pair, on and off the track.

The public had now started to take an interest in a possible rivalry and they met again at the 1978 European Championships in Prague. Peter Coe encouraged his son to go out fast and he clocked 49.32 seconds for the first 400 metres. It was a pace that he couldn't maintain, however. East Germany's Olaf Beyer went on to win and Ovett also overtook Coe, beating his British record in the process. (When East German secret-police records were released after the fall of the Berlin Wall, Beyer's name was on a list of athletes supposed to have been involved in doping programmes, although he has denied taking performance-enhancing substances.)

Coe was clearly hurt by the miscalculation, because he promptly reclaimed the record two weeks later by dipping under 1 minute 44 seconds. Later that year he proved he could also mix it with the best over longer distances, when he won a four-mile road race in record time, beating established runners like Eamonn Coghlan and Mike McLeod.

Coe was now entering his peak years. In 1979 he set three world records – the 800 metres and the mile in Oslo, and the 1500 metres in Zurich – in just six weeks. He was the first man to hold all three records and he backed them up with wins in the European Cup 800 metres in Turin, anchoring the British 4x400-metre relay team with the fastest split, and remaining undefeated over any distance for the entire year. He was ranked number one in both main distances and was voted athlete of the year by *Athletics Weekly* and *Track & Field News*.

Ovett was also improving over various distances. He ran a new personal best in the 800 metres in 1978 and backed it up with a two-mile world best that eclipsed the great Kenyan distance runner, Henry Rono. Had he concentrated on the pacemaker-led Grand Prix events, he would have undoubtedly challenged for more honours, but he was building nicely towards the big one two years hence.

The pair were both picked for the Great Britain squad for the 1980 Olympics in Moscow and when the Games finally arrived all the talk was about them. "It wasn't the Moscow Olympics," said Dave Moorcroft. "It was the Coe-Ovett Olympics."

They came to the Games in good form. Coe was the world record-holder in the 800 metres and he was the heavy favourite going into the event (just prior to the Games he actually held world records over 800, 1000 and 1500 metres, as well as the best mile time, although Ovett broke his world record for the latter an hour later). Ovett, on the other hand, had switched his allegiance and his preference now lay with the longer of the two Olympic middle-distances.

In the 800-metre final Coe began as clear favourite. But as the race began he looked unsettled and didn't set his usual pace, and the two men were towards the back of the field at the end of the first lap. When Ovett kicked with 200 metres to go, Coe was back in fifth and looked to be struggling as the pace increased. Ovett's powerful run for home took him into the lead midway down the home straight while Coe was still back in fourth. Despite a strong last 50 metres and a desperate lunge for the line, Coe had been tactically outmanoeuvred and could only take silver. Ovett's broad smile on the rostrum was in direct contrast to the desolate and shattered look on Coe's face. He was a broken man, but he needed to recover fast.

"It's not unusual to have great sporting head-to-heads, but what was uncommon was this rivalry was between two people from the same country who were chasing the same spoils at the same time, and that was a big added pressure." Sebastian Coe

It was another week until the 1500 metres and the press were now talking down Coe's chances. However, the criticism seemed to galvanise Coe and he became consumed with avenging the defeat. The 1500 metres was Ovett's strongest discipline however (he hadn't been beaten over the distance in his senior career) and despite finding motivation harder to come by now his desire for Olympic gold had been sated, he was odds-on for a historic double. The stage was set for Ovett to be crowned the greatest middle distance runner in the world, not to mention the most decorated British athlete.

The first two laps of the final were slow but then the pace increased dramatically. There was no doubt that this favoured Coe because it had effectively turned the race into two warm-up laps and an 800 metres. When they rounded the final bend and hit the home straight Coe was in the lead but Ovett was on his shoulder and looking to kick for the line. This time Coe wasn't going to be denied. He put in a final spurt that broke Ovett, the latter fading to finish third. Coe threw his arms up in a mixture of ecstasy and redemption before collapsing to the track. Unbeaten over this distance for three years and 45 races, on the biggest stage of all, Ovett could only take the bronze.

It had been an epic race and, thanks to the enthralling Moscow stalemate, the wider world now knew all about the rivalry between the pair. Coe came away from Moscow with mixed emotions, however. He'd been beaten over his favourite distance but had exacted revenge in Ovett's speciality.

"Looking back, we were good for one other. We trained that little bit harder and then went for it in our championship meetings." Sebastian Coe

Despite 1981 being the finest year for both men, it passed without their paths crossing. Coe was in superb form and he began by taking the indoor 800-metre world record. He then tore up the record books completely. In Florence in June he ran 1.41.73 outdoors to set a mark that wouldn't be beaten for 16 years (it is still the third fastest time in history), and he then set the 1000 metres record with a time that stood for 19 years and has only been bettered once since.

He promptly won the Europa Cup 800 metres, set a new personal best in the 1500 metres and twice broke the world record for the mile (lowering it to 3.47.33) before ending the season with gold over 800 metres at the World Cup in Rome. As in 1979, he was unbeaten over any distance for the entire season and he was duly named athlete of the year.

If 1980 and 1981 had seen the high points of a remarkable career to date, the next two years, with a couple of minor exceptions, represented the lows. Coe was injured for much of the summer but he still managed to break the 4x800-metre world record (with Peter Elliott, Garry Cook and Steve Cram) with a time that stood for 24 years. He only won silver at the 1982 European Championships, although the team later revealed that he'd been suffering from glandular fever.

Then, despite breaking a couple of indoor world records early in 1983, Coe was laid up for the remainder of the season with a severe bout of toxoplasmosis, a parasitic disease characterised by flu-like symptoms. He only returned to training in spring the following year which gave him precious little time to prepare for his second Olympic Games.

Ovett's inter-Olympic years precisely mirrored Coe's. He was also at his peak in 1981 and the pair exchanged world records in the mile three times in ten days. The fact that they didn't meet on the track throughout the season has raised some eyebrows but it seems that they could earn more for their appearances and in prize money if they avoided each other, because they would both be the stars of their respective meets and were more likely to win against lesser opposition.

Ovett saw it differently, believing that because their seasons didn't coincide (he was doing hundreds of miles of cross-country, while Coe was sharpening his track work), Coe would have wiped him out early on in each year and he didn't want to compete at a disadvantage. The public didn't seem to mind and the media revelled in a rivalry that was never far from the back pages.

With Coe not running in Oslo, Ovett was hot favourite for the 1500 metres, and pacemaker Tom Byers set off so quickly that the chasing pack simply listened for their split times and waited for him to tire. Sadly, the remaining athletes were not being given the correct timing information and Byers found himself ten seconds ahead at the start of the final lap. Instead of pulling out, he decided to continue and, despite chasing him down, Ovett could only take silver.

The following season Ovett's progress was hampered by a twisted knee and several more injuries, and he didn't return until 1983. He wasn't selected for the 800 metres at the World Championships in Helsinki and ran a poor 1500 to finish in fourth. But he soon bounced back with a world 1500 metres record in Rieti and was only just pipped to the post by Steve Cram in an epic mile at Crystal Palace. He then headed to Australia for his winter training before the Los Angeles Olympics.

The 1984 Games were supposed to represent the culmination of two great careers. Both men had had their problems in the build up but they were now back to their best. And then Ovett developed bronchitis and his world caved in. He desperately tried to compete in the 800 metres but he was suffering severe respiratory problems. Despite this, he battled his way through the heats and only qualified for the final with a desperate lunge for the line, after which he practically collapsed with exhaustion.

Coe's route to the final had been relatively easy by comparison and he lined up for the final in the Los Angeles Coliseum feeling far more confident than the reigning champion. The first lap was brisk but Coe and Ovett were both in contention behind noted front runner, the Brazilian Joaquim Cruz. By the time they hit the back straight it was clear that Ovett was in trouble and he faded completely on the final turn. This left Coe and Cruz to battle it out for glory. Cruz finished like the Coe of 1981, however, blowing the rest of the field away with a superb sprint finish. Coe battled hard but could only take the silver.

Ovett collapsed again and had to spend two nights in hospital but he eventually recovered and somehow managed to make it through his 1500-metre heats to reach yet another final. In typically robust fashion he ignored the advice of friends, family and experts and took his place on the track alongside Coe and Cram.

The three British athletes were content to keep amongst the pack for the first two laps but by the time they came to the bell the field had spread a little. Coe was now in second with Cram third and Ovett fourth. However, the question for Ovett was not whether he could win but whether he could finish. His illness caught up with him at the beginning of the last lap, however, and he was forced to pull out (he had to be taken away on a stretcher after suffering severe chest pains). With 200 metres to go, Coe kicked hard and took the lead but Cram wasn't easy to shake and he shadowed Coe around the final turn. Coe kicked again into the home straight and appeared to relax at the same time. His style was so fluid that he seemed to be running on air. It was a glorious moment and Cram couldn't match his blistering speed.

As Coe crossed the finish line he roared in unbridled euphoria at the press box, full to the brim of people who had written him off in the run-up to the race. The reigning champion was now the first man to retain an Olympic 1500-metre title, and he had done so in emphatic style,

Ovett's career never really recovered and he couldn't reach the heights of Moscow and the record-breaking years immediately thereafter. Coe, too, was winding down, although he took 800-metre gold at the 1986 European Championships in Stuttgart, his only major title at what was probably his best distance (he won silver in the 1500 behind Cram). He failed to qualify for the 1988 Olympics after picking up a chest infection and he retired in 1990. Ovett had been concentrating on longer distances but a run of poor results saw him retire the following year. With Peter Elliot and Steve Cram narrowly missing out on gold in Seoul, the African nations became the dominant force over the middle distances.

The Ovett-Coe rivalry elevated the status of both British middle-distance running and athletics as a spectator sport, and a host of superb British runners followed in their wake. But it was these two great men who delivered the standout performances at major championships. They captured the public imagination with their rivalry and dragged the sport into a modern, professional age.

"I loved to watch Coe run. I got the impression he and Ovett were real enemies, but I think they would have lowered all their world records had they raced more often." Arne Andersson

With their careers a distant memory and their friendship cemented, their views on each other are now delivered with the utmost respect and honesty. Coe considers Ovett "the most naturally talented athlete I ever raced against, by a distance," while Ovett considers Coe "without question the greatest middle-distance runner we have had in the UK". The ultimate accolades from the finest all-British athletics rivalry.

Verdict: There is no doubt that Coe was the more elegant runner, his laidback and fluid style easy on the eye and on the track. Ovett was more muscular and not afraid to mix it up in the midfield but this brawn allied with great tactical nous was usually enough to see off the best. Only Coe at his peak remained out of reach and he takes it by a nose.

Borg and McEnroe before the 1980 Wimbledon final

McEnroe may have won the epic
tie-break but Borg took the match

The two great rivals share another
moment on centre court

Palmer and Nicklaus in their prime

The King in his US Coastguard days

The Golden Bear's last appearance at Augusta

The mock obituary for English cricket in *The Times*

Bill Woodfull ducks a Larwood bouncer in the Brisbane Test
during the infamous 'Bodyline' series in 1933

The Greatest. Australia's Don Bradman guides
the ball past Godfrey Evans and Bill Edrich at
Trent Bridge on the 1948 Invincibles' Tour

The coveted Ashes Urn in the museum at Lord's

England captain Andrew Strauss leads the celebrations after the 2010-11 series win

The end of the infamous 'No mas' fight

Leonard

Hagler

Hearns

Duran

Steve Ovett wins the Olympic 800-metre title in Moscow in 1980

A despondent Coe can hardly bear to congratulate Ovett

Seb Coe leads Steve Cram and Steve
Ovett at the Los Angeles Olympics in 1984

Revenge is sweet. Coe wins the 1500 metres in Moscow ahead
of his great rival

The Boat Race course

The annual race is one of London's main tourist attractions

The Cambridge crew on the left fall half a length behind
Oxford at the Chiswick Pier in the 2010 Boat Race

Activist Trenton Oldfield causes the 2012 race to be
suspended after swimming into Oxford's path

The first State of Origin Shield with
Queensland's Wally Lewis and Brett
Kenny from New South Wales

The Ron McAuliffe Medal

The Cockroaches prepare to take on the Cane Toads

Trent Barrett hits Steve Price in game two of the
2009 series at the ANZ Stadium in Sydney

The first game of the 2012 series is marred by an all-in brawl

Evert with the Wimbledon Trophy

The pair line up for the 1982 Wimbledon final

Martina Navratilova is immortalised
on a Paraguayan stamp

After 15 years battling it out across the net, the rivals
finally become friends

The Boat Race

On March 12th 1829, a Cambridge student and member of the new Cambridge University Boat Club, Charles Merivale, challenged schoolfriend Charles Wordsworth, who was studying at Oxford, to assemble a crew for a boat race along the Thames at Henley in Oxfordshire. Having taken their colours from their stroke-man's college (Christ Church), the Oxford Crew turned up in their now-familiar dark blue outfits, while the Cambridge crew wore pink sashes. Oxford emerged as comfortable victors after the race had to be re-started. However, such was the success of the event – twenty thousand people turned up to watch – that the people of Henley decided to hold their own annual regatta, a tradition that continues today.

The second race wasn't held until 1836, by which time Cambridge had adopted the light blue duck-egg colours of Eton. The venue had changed however, the course starting at Westminster and ending at Putney, a distance of 5¾ miles. In the years that followed, the universities couldn't agree where to stage the race, with Oxford preferring Henley and Cambridge wanting London.

By 1839 the Oxford University Boat Club had been formed and racing between the universities resumed. The tradition of the captain of the losing eight challenging the winner to a race the following year continues to this day. Up until 1842, the Westminster course was used, but when that became too congested the start was moved six miles upstream to what was then a village in the suburbs: Putney.

The championship course from Putney to Mortlake was first run in 1845. It is marked by the University Boat Race Stones on the south bank and is 4 miles and 374 yards (6779 metres) long. Although the race is run upstream against the river's flow, the start always coincides with an incoming flood tide that generates powerful and favourable currents in deep water. However, in 1846, 1856, 1862 and 1863 the race was run in reverse from

Mortlake to Putney.

Before the race, the rowing clubs' presidents toss the 1829 sovereign to decide which crew has the right to choose stations. The northern Middlesex station has the inside line on the first and last bends, said to be worth a third-of-a-length each, while the southern Surrey station takes the shorter line for the longer middle bend at St Paul's School, said to be worth about a length. The weather also plays a part in deciding which station to choose. If there is a strong westerly breeze blowing against the incoming tide, the river can become choppy in deeper water. Indeed, conditions have occasionally been so poor that one or both boats have sunk – Oxford in 1925 and 1951, Cambridge in 1859 and 1978, and both in 1912, when the race was rerun in more favourable conditions the following day.

Having chosen stations, the boats are then anchored to two moored stake boats so that their bows line up with the stones. The coxes must keep an arm raised while their crews get into position. When both have lowered their arms to indicate they are ready, the umpire waves a red flag to start the race. Immediately after the start, the crew on the Middlesex side try to hold the centre line of the river where the flood tide flows faster. With both boats vying for an early lead, they often come together and their oars frequently clash. In 2001 the umpire had to halt the race to separate the eights.

The crews race past the historic boathouses on the Putney Embankment before heading into the first Middlesex bend, which takes them past Craven Cottage, Fulham's football stadium. A stone monument to rowing coach, Cambridge oarsman and founder of the Head of the River race, Steve Fairbairn, marks the first mile and is traditionally used as a timing point. For the next two miles the bend favours the crew on the Surrey side. They pass the Harrods Repository before reaching the Hammersmith Road Bridge on the apex of the bend. In around eight out of ten races, the boat that leads at the bridge, which is just before the halfway point, goes on to win.

The course now moves into a section known as the Chiswick Reach, at the end of which are the Chiswick Steps, which are used as another timing marker. The Surrey bend then gradually straightens out, before easing into the final Middlesex turn. The deepest water is directly down the river's centre and the crews will again compete for the fastest line. If a south-westerly wind picks up while the boats are in this stretch, it runs against the flood tide and causes the water to become quite choppy. Indeed, it is here that the Cambridge boat sank in 1978.

They then head underneath Barnes Railway Bridge. The boat leading at the bridge almost always goes on to win. Only in 1952 and 2002 has the trailing crew fought back to take the honours. They then pass the Mortlake Brewery on the Surrey bank, before crossing the finish line just downstream from Chiswick Road Bridge. The course record of 16 minutes and 19 seconds was set by Cambridge in 1998 when they fielded the tallest and heaviest crew in Boat Race history. The victorious 2005 Oxford crew broke the weight record, however.

Such is the perceived prestige of the race that the universities have reportedly stooped to breaking the strict rules on qualification. No sports scholarships are awarded by the institutions, so their rowers must gain admission via their academic credentials, although whether all the top athletes have achieved the required grades has caused the odd argument. There is also much fodder for pub debate about how well the crews would stand up against international competition. Most regattas, like the long-distance Olympic events, take place over 2000 metres, but the Boat Race takes in over four miles of the ever-changing Thames. The crews, therefore, have to train for this longer distance early in the season.

Between September and December, the rowers are put through a rigorous training and selection process by their coaches. Those who can't keep up with their academic studies are often forced to drop out. In December the coaches will draw up a list of two trial eights. They will compete against one another on the championship course to assess their progress. As the crews are divided into the Blue and reserve eights, they are then pitted against top club and international squads. (On race day, the reserve boats – Isis for Oxford and Goldie for Cambridge – go out first.)

Although the lengths of the warm-up races varies, the university crews are usually competitive, although some of the opposing crews have not been together very long. An experienced Oxford crew only lost out to a German national eight by a third of a length at Henley in 2005, and a Cambridge crew set the fastest time in the 2007 Head of the River race before the event was cancelled due to poor weather.

There have been two cases of mutiny before the event. By the winter of 1958, Oxford had a talented and settled squad, including Yale oarsmen Charlie Grimes, a gold medallist at the Melbourne Olympics two years earlier, and Reed Rubin. The president of the boat club, Ronnie Howard, had rowed for Isis under coach Hugh Edwards in a boat that had consistently outperformed the Blue eight, so he, naturally, appointed Edwards as the coach for the main event. Employing strict codes of behaviour and training, Edwards proved to be a controversial coaching choice and both Grimes and Rubin backed out of the eight. They then, somewhat controversially, announced that they would form a rival eight that would race Howard's boat for the right to face Cambridge. Howard retaliated by first winning a vote of confidence in his eight and then beating Cambridge in the race by six lengths.

The second mutiny also concerned the Oxford boat. In 1987, five Americans withdrew from the squad because one of them had been dropped in favour of Scotsman Donald Macdonald, who, although he wanted a seat guaranteed, had lost in a trial against Chris Clark, one of the American oarsmen. Oxford called upon Isis for help and with a depleted team they still managed to win the race. Although controversial coach Dan Topolski had borne the brunt of the criticism in the lead-up to the race, he masterminded their victory by bucking conventional wisdom and instructing the squad to stay out of the choppy deeper water.

Aside from Olympic gold medallists Matthew Pinsent, Tim Foster, Luka Grubor, Kieran West, Ed Coode and Andrew Lindsay, many other famous oarsmen have graced the race. George Mallory's climbing partner on their ill-fated 1924 expedition to Mount Everest, Andrew 'Sandy' Irvine, competed for Oxford in 1922 and 1923; Antony Armstrong-Jones, the Earl of Snowdon, raced in 1950; Lord Moynihan coxed Oxford to victory in 1977; and even Bertie Wooster himself, Hugh Laurie, rowed for Cambridge in 1980.

Today, the race is watched by an estimated quarter-of-a-million people on the banks of the Thames and by nearly ten million on television in the UK alone. At the time of writing, the score stands at 81 victories to Cambridge and 76 to Oxford, with a single but controversial dead heat in 1877, when, it is rumoured in Oxford, the judge, 'Honest' John Phelps had fallen asleep under a bush at the finish and had to give the result as a draw. Although they mischievously refer to the result as a dead heat to Oxford by four feet, contemporary accounts disagree with the myth, this from *The Times*:

'Oxford, partially disabled, were making effort after effort to hold their rapidly waning lead, while Cambridge, who, curiously enough, had settled together again, and were rowing almost as one man, were putting on a magnificent spurt at 40 strokes to the minute, with a view to catching their opponents before reaching the winning-post. Thus struggling over the remaining portion of the course, the two eights raced past the flag alongside one another, and the gun fired amid a scene of excitement rarely equalled and never exceeded. Cheers for one crew were succeeded by counter-cheers for the other, and it was impossible to tell what the result was until the press boat backed down to the judge and inquired the issue. John Phelps, the waterman, who officiated, replied that the noses of the boats passed the post strictly level, and that the result was a dead heat.'

Close finishes are a feature of the race. Oxford won by a canvas (approximately four feet) in 1952 and 1980, and they won again, this time by a foot, in 2003 when Cambridge's star oarsman Wayne Pommen had to be replaced at the last minute after suffering an injury in a warm-up race. The previous year, Cambridge were holding a comfortable lead when Sebastian Mayer collapsed with exhaustion only a few hundred yards from the finish. Oxford stormed through to win by three-quarters of a length.

In 2004, the crews repeatedly clashed oars and Oxford's bowman was unseated. Cambridge managed to survive the onslaught and went on to win. Oxford had their revenge two years later in heavy rain. They decided to use a pump to remove excess water from the bottom of the boat but Cambridge went without. It was the right decision. Cambridge became overloaded and Oxford won.

In 2007 Cambridge were strong favourites. They boasted five returning Blues and had a wealth of international experience. Although the lighter Oxford crew pushed them all the way, by the Chiswick Steps Cambridge had a slender lead. Even with the extra weight and tidier technique, they only managed to win by a shade over a length.

The 2010 race promised to be close because the eights were well matched in age, height, weight and experience. Oxford started strongly from the Surrey station and forced Cambridge to row the slower line around Hammersmith Bridge and the Chiswick Eyot. Cambridge rallied and finally overtook the Oxford boat at Barnes Bridge, a lead they held until the finish line.

In 2012, the 158th race became front page news around the world when it had to be stopped for nearly half an hour after environmental and anti-elitist campaigner Trenton Oldfield dived into the river and swam between the two crews near Chiswick Pier. Until that point the race had been finely balanced, with Oxford fighting hard to maintain their quarter-length lead over a Cambridge eight that was just feeling the benefit of the Surrey bend. Assistant Umpire Sir Matthew Pinsent suddenly spotted Oldfield in the water and his superior, John Garrett, instructed both crews to stop racing. He made the decision to restart from the eastern end of the Chiswick Eyot after Oldfield had been taken away and charged under the Public Order Act.

The boats clashed almost immediately after the restart as the Oxford eight tried to cut across and get position in the deeper part of the river but the move backfired when Hanno Wienhausen's oar broke. Garrett believed Oxford were responsible for the clash so allowed the race to continue. Cambridge then eased clear to win by four lengths but the drama wasn't over. Oxford's bowman Alex Woods had expended so much energy that he collapsed immediately after the race and had to be taken to Charing Cross Hospital. The awards ceremony was cancelled and the winning crew were not given a time due to the mid-race delay. Thankfully, Woods made a complete recovery.

Cambridge enjoyed 13 consecutive victories between 1924 and 1936, while Oxford's best run of wins was 10 between 1976 and 1985. This was a period of dominance for the dark blues because they won every race bar two between 1974 and 1992. Since 1989 both universities have won 12 times.

The race is the oldest amateur event of national importance in the UK, and it remains the world's most famous student sports event. Television audiences compare favourably with five of the UK's great sporting occasions: the Grand National, the men's singles final at Wimbledon, the Derby, the British Grand Prix and the FA Cup final. Worldwide TV audiences vary from 20 million to over 400 million.

Thankfully for the spectator, the race has remained largely unchanged throughout its 165-year history. Today it is still a private and fiercely amateur event for 18 men (and occasionally women) between the world's most famous universities, and it is the basis for a unique rivalry that has made an indelible mark on the world of sport.

Verdict: Oxford made the early running but Cambridge have closed the gap. The two crews remain tied at 12 victories each over the last 24 years so it can only be a dead heat.

State of Origin

In the middle of every domestic Australian rugby league season since 1980, a best-of-three-match series has been played between the Queensland Maroons and the New South Wales Blues, and for more than 30 bruising but memorable years this series has developed into Australian sport's greatest rivalry, no mean feat for a country synonymous with sporting endeavour and passion. The fiercely contested 2012 series was one of the finest of recent times, with Queensland snatching the deciding game by a single point to seal a seventh consecutive title.

However, the real story began back in 1908, the year the Australian Rugby League was founded, when representative sides from the two states met at Sydney's Agricultural Ground. Sadly, the game did not reflect well on the combatants, with New South Wales handing their opponents a 43-0 drubbing. Some observers believed the match was a waste of time and should be discontinued but the states persevered.

The Blues dominated the early years, apart from a brief Queensland resurgence in the mid-1920s when they won 11 of 12 matches. In 1925 a team – nicknamed the Kangaroos – was selected to tour Great Britain, but the tour was cancelled at the last minute because the Rugby Football League felt that the New Zealanders would provide sterner opposition. Apart from during the two world wars, this was the only period when tours to the UK were cancelled, and the Australian Rugby League Board of Control was rightly annoyed that they had been overlooked by the mother country.

The decision was all the more strange given that the Maroons had just mauled the Maoris home and away, causing some to speculate that the Blues were partly responsible for the RFL cancelling the tour because they didn't want a side representing Australia to be largely composed of Queenslanders. The Maroons believed the conspiracy theory and this is one of the underlying reasons why the tribal rivalry is so intense 80 years on.

In 1956, poker machines were legalised in all registered rugby league clubs in New South Wales. This gave the clubs a huge revenue stream, which they used to attract the best players. A number of high-profile Queenslanders were tempted south by big-money contracts and, when they were deemed eligible to play for the Blues, the gap was soon reflected on the pitch. Before the machines had been introduced, Queensland, although often outplayed, still managed to win a quarter of all the interstate series. Between 1956 and 1981, they won just once, in 1959.

This imbalance of power led to a fall in spectator numbers and a loss of interest in the contest as a spectacle. Matches were inexplicably staged at small grounds in the middle of the week (apparently so as not to interfere with club football in Sydney) and, in 1977, New South Wales actually refused to host their rivals. (It was around this time that the Blues got the nickname of the 'Cockroaches' and the Reds the 'Cane Toads'.)

It fell to former Australian Vice-Captain Jack Reardon, Brisbane reporter Hugh Lunn, co-founder of the Brisbane Broncos, Barry Maranta, and Wayne Reid (Maranta's business partner) to try to salvage the game. They approached the President of Queensland Rugby League, Senator Ron McAuliffe, and suggested that Sydney-based Queenslanders (who had been lured south by the poker machine money) could be coerced into representing their original state in a Test Match selection trial. McAuliffe was initially sceptical, because he was concerned that the contest would be degraded if the recalled players were then thrashed in the opening fixture.

Three clubs – St George Dragons, South Sydney Rabbitohs and the Eastern Suburbs Roosters – refused to release their players anyway, but Kevin Humphreys, then President of the New South Wales Rugby League saw the value of revitalising the series and threatened to make the match an official Test trial, which meant the clubs would be forced to release the players. The clubs were left with no option but to back down.

In 1980, two interstate matches were played under the old rules, which New South Wales won convincingly in front of small crowds. It seemed the concept was dead in the water, but

McAuliffe convinced the league to sanction a third game under the new 'origin' (you play for the state of your birth) rules and then set about selling tickets as if his life depended on it.

McAuliffe can rightly claim to be the saviour of the contest, and he also pioneered a number of new training methods, including the adoption of sports nutrition, employing specialist doctors, and bullying sponsors until he got the right deal for the players, fans and TV networks.

The third game saw Rod Morris, Kerry Boustead and Rod Reddy (amongst several other high-profile players) swap their Blue club colours for the Queensland Maroon of their birth state (a rule that was later changed to the state where they had first played at Under-16 level) and, at a Lang Park Stadium (now the Suncorp Stadium) in Brisbane that was packed to its 33,000 capacity, Artie Beetson led the Maroons to a historic 20-10 victory. The score only told part of the story, however. The match itself was as brutal as it was brilliant.

After 23 minutes, Maroon halfback Greg Oliphant administered a little facial massage to Blues second rower Graham Wynn while the latter was on the ground after a tackle. Wynn rose to his feet and returned the favour with interest in the form of a decent left hook which, when Beetson intervened to defend his halfback, sparked an all-in brawl, whereupon both sides traded hits with customary enthusiasm. English referee Billy Thompson was quite used to the game descending into fisticuffs, so he let the players cool down for a minute before restarting with a scrum.

The Maroons settled into a rhythm and came close to scoring several times, before Mal Meninga combined with Chris Close to put Kerry Boustead over. Meninga converted to give the Maroons a 9-3 lead, although the Blues pulled a penalty back by half-time and only went in 9-5 down. A darting run by Chris Close resulted in a try, and the conversion and two Meninga penalties saw the Maroons ease into a 13-point lead. Despite scoring a try and hammering at the Maroon defence in the last ten minutes, a final Meninga penalty sealed the victory over the Blues in the first State of Origin match, a match that changed the course of rugby league in Australia forever.

The following season's results mirrored those in 1980, with

the Blues winning the first two matches under the old selection rules. The third match of the series was played under origin rules and, once again, it proved to be a cracker. New South Wales were clearly smarting from the previous year and charged into a 15-0 lead after only 27 minutes. But the inspirational Meninga and Artie Beetson (who now coached the side) read the Maroons the riot act at the break and they rallied with tries of their own to level the score. There were only two minutes left on the clock when Meninga kicked the ball through towards the Blues line and gave chase. He was tackled before he had re-gathered it and New Zealander Kevin Steele awarded a penalty try. Meninga then converted to give his side a narrow victory.

The pressure was now on to change the way the entire series was played as it was clear that the origin matches were more popular and the standard was arguably even higher than in the traditional interstate games. Indeed, the TV ratings had actually surpassed Australian Rules Football in its southern state capital strongholds. But on the field the balance of power was shifting again.

By 1982 it was agreed that all three interstate matches would be played under State of Origin rules for the now-famous shield. This time the teams wouldn't have to worry about changing their line-ups and formations halfway through a series, so they both had ample preparation time. There was trouble in the Maroon camp, however. Several Brisbane youngsters were looking to secure lucrative contracts in Sydney, so the management presented them with an ultimatum: sign for Brisbane for another year or they would never play for Queensland. The players reluctantly backed down but the incident created unnecessary tension in the build-up to the series.

The Blues took an early lead but a Meninga-inspired fight-back was always on the cards and the Lang Park faithful were near hysterical by the end. The fairytale wasn't to be however, and the Maroons went down 20-16. Usually gracious in defeat, Senator McAuliffe had a swipe at the New South Wales structure by saying that they hadn't released all of the players the Maroons needed, and his comments had the desired effect. State of Origin was fast developing into the sporting world's most brutal rivalry.

The second encounter saw the Maroons take an early lead and they held on to win a low-scoring match. Both teams made a number of surprise selections for the deciding match at the Sydney Cricket Ground (which was at least half full). The game was extremely hard-fought and a number of brawls broke out, but the defences came out on top and the Maroons won 10-5. Whereas the interstate matches had been played mid-week in front of only a few thousand fans, the gates were now in excess of 20,000 for every match and more than three million domestic fans watched the series on television. McAuliffe's grand plan seemed to be working. Rugby League was once again the top spectator sport in Australia.

The Queensland Maroons made all the early running in the first few years of the origin series, but by 1985 the Blues, under inspirational captain Steve Mortimer, were a different proposition. Newcastle, a city up the coast from Sydney, had been linked to the state capital by superhighway and it was a hotbed of league talent. Now that they were able to draw on these previously untapped resources, the Blues fielded a strong side in the 1985 series.

A crowd of 33,000 saw them demolish their northern rivals 18-2, which must have seemed like abject humiliation for the Maroons given that it came after four years of utter dominance. The Blues and their faithful fans finally embraced Origin when nearly 40,000 packed into the SCG two weeks later. They weren't to be disappointed: the Blues scored three tries to two and took the series with a 21-14 victory. In most sporting contests a two-nil lead in a three-match series leads to a disappointing final match in a dead rubber, not so with Origin bragging rights up for grabs.

Although he no longer had any official capacity with the Maroons, Ron McAuliffe popped into their dressing room before the final match of the 1985 series: "We may have been beaten 2-0 but it isn't too late to salvage the reputation of Queensland Rugby League and of Queensland itself. We'll be regarded as a team of whingers if you don't go out onto the paddock and do them over."

The team were inspired and salvaged their reputations with a convincing 20-6 win. The Blues had no answer to their total commitment (which occasionally bordered on GBH), but no amount of violence could detract from a solid offensive performance.

The following year marked a low point for the Maroons. Although they were competitive in every fixture, they were narrowly beaten in all three, handing the Blues the first series whitewash. The Maroons returned in 1987 with a strong side (despite Meninga being out injured for the entire series) but they still lost a tight opening encounter at Lang Park. The second game was played in appalling conditions at the SCG, but a record crowd of 42,000 turned out to watch the Queenslanders level the series after an epic match. The decider was another closely fought contest that saw the Maroons squeeze home 10-8.

Sensing that the series was attracting the attention of the wider sporting world, a fourth match was added to the calendar, but it was scheduled to take place in Long Beach, California, so that the game could be showcased to an American audience. The Maroons knew the trophy was safely in their hands for another year, so they tried to drink the bar dry on the flight over. The Blues, however, were still smarting and resolved to treat the unofficial match as a series decider. Ticket sales were poor, so several thousand college students were allowed in free. The New South Wales soft drink policy clearly worked as the Blues beat a rather tired Queensland team 30-18. The experiment was not a great success and the tour has not been reprised since. (The game was finally given official status in 2003.)

The newly formed Brisbane Broncos controversially entered the New South Wales state competition in 1988. They enjoyed a good start to the season and contributed most of the team to face the Blues in that year's Origin series. Queensland promptly completed their first whitewash, to the delight of Ron McAuliffe. Sadly, the great champion of Maroon Rugby League died seven weeks later from a stroke. How he would have enjoyed Queensland's second clean sweep the following year.

Many high-profile Maroons retired in the early 1990s and the balance of power moved south once more. The New South Wales outfit decided to go with a strong forward pack to try to dominate the Maroons. This led to the matches becoming much more physical, with less emphasis on the flowing, running rugby that had wowed the crowds in the 1980s. The middle years of the decade also saw the emergence of the Super League, and a war over who controlled the broadcasting rights.

The key players were Rupert Murdoch's Super League (Australia), which was backed by his News Corporation empire, and a rival faction in the form of Kerry Packer's Optus Vision-backed Australian Rugby League. Competition for the broadcasting rights was really about controlling the amount of rugby league that would be shown on television. This exposure would attract more sponsors and ultimately lead to complete control over the sport in Australia, so there was plenty to fight for.

Murdoch lured several clubs away from the ARL administrators and formed a rival league in 1997. The split caused confusion amongst fans and TV audiences tailed off. Thankfully, both sides eventually saw sense and the following year ARL invited the Super League teams to join them in a single National Rugby League that was joint-owned by both parties. The TV rights were handed to Packer's Channel 9 Network for AUS$13 million per year until 2007, while the free-to-air rights were renegotiated for an annual AUS$40 million until 2012.

The improvements in broadcasting technology, such as high-definition, interactive and 3D capabilities, have brought renewed interest in the rivalry from satellite stations and the matches are now shown around the world. In 1999, a record crowd of 88,336 crammed into Stadium Australia in Sydney for the first match of that year's series.

The 2012 series was perhaps the most exciting of all and it broke both attendance and TV viewing records. Game one was held at the end of May at the Etihad Stadium in Melbourne in front of 56,000 fans and 2.5 million TV viewers. The New South Wales Blues made the early running and Akuila Uate recovered a high kick to score a try in the sixth minute. As is customary in these highly charged clashes, a brawl soon followed and Blues centre Michael Jennings was sin-binned for punching Brent Tate. Darius Boyd then scored two tries for the Maroons to give them a 12-4 lead at the break. Jennings scored a try for the Blues shortly after the restart, but the Maroons resisted the subsequent onslaught and scored a late, albeit controversial, try through Greg Inglis to seal an 18-10 victory.

The second match was, if anything, even more physical. Held at the ANZ Stadium in Sydney in front of 83,000, it recorded the highest TV ratings for any second match in Origin history. The Blues led after a Brett Stewart try, but the Maroons went into the break ahead after Ben Hannant went over. When Cooper Cronk was sin-binned early in the second half for a professional foul, the Blues rammed home their man advantage and scored two tries from line breaks. Despite a late rally, Queensland couldn't claw back the deficit and they lost 16-12.

The deciding game in front of 53,000 at Brisbane's Suncorp Stadium was an absolute cracker and it broke the record for the highest ever audience figures for a rugby league match. Plus, to further emphasise just how popular this rivalry had become it was also the second most watched programme in Australian TV history.

Brett Morris ran in the first try of the match in the 13th minute, which, when added to an early Todd Carney penalty, gave the Blues an 8-0 lead. But glorious tries from Darius Boyd, Jonathan Thurston and Justin Hodges saw Queensland enter the break 16-8 up.

Early in the second half Brett Stewart pounced on a loose ball and Carney converted to bring the Blues to within two points, but Thurston kicked two penalties to extend the lead by six to 20-14. With ten minutes on the clock, Robbie Farah chipped a beautiful cross-field kick into the Maroons in-goal area and Josh Morris out-jumped Daruis Boyd to score a magnificent try. Carney converted from the touchline to tie the match but a last-gasp Cronk field goal saw the Maroons snatch a one-point victory, securing the Queenslanders a record seventh consecutive Origin series. The Maroons have now won 21 series (and 51 matches overall) to the Blues 12 series and 43 matches.

There can be no doubt that the physicality of the players, the pace of the game, and the level of excitement have all contributed to making rugby league one of the most compelling sports. Indeed, it is no exaggeration to suggest that the State of Origin series is one of the most ferocious and tribal sporting rivalries on the planet.

Verdict: Historically, Queensland have won more games and series, and the Reds have also been dominant for much of the last decade. The Cane Toads take the spoils.

Chris Evert

vs

Martina Navratilova

Women's tennis had long been viewed as dull and of poor quality by some of the male players – indeed Fred Stolle claimed that no one would pay to watch them play, and Stan Smith said tennis de-feminised women and wasn't good for them – but the rivalry between Chris Evert and Martina Navratilova elevated the profile of the women's game and provided the spectator with 16 years of unparalleled entertainment. With Billie Jean King cracking the whip, women's tennis evolved from the polite hitting of the country club into the hard-hitting and pressure-laden duels that defined the era.

This is a story about two players who desperately wanted the same thing, who found their way blocked by one another, and who eventually forged a friendship that allowed them to forgive each other for all the on-court heartbreak.

The two first met across the net in 1973. Evert was 18 years old, Navratilova just 16. Navratilova's only goal for that first match was to get Evert to remember her name – she did, the two chatting amiably at the next event in St Petersburg, Florida. Eighty matches later, of which a scarcely believable 60 were finals, the two played their last game, and so ended one of the greatest rivalries in the history of sport. By way of comparison, Björn Borg and John McEnroe only met 14 times. And when boxing enthusiasts mutter about Muhammad Ali-Joe Frazier being the biggest sporting rivalry, Navratilova casually reminds them that the two great heavyweights only met three times in the ring.

Chris Evert was born in Fort Lauderdale, Florida. Her father, Jimmy, was a professional coach who had won a number of minor tournaments. He started teaching Chris the basics when she was just five years old and by 1969 she was the top-ranked under-14 girl in the United States. It wasn't all plain sailing, though. She also enjoyed swimming and initially resented her father's decision to push her towards tennis. In the long run, however, it was clearly the right choice, although to begin with she was more concerned with how well she played rather than if she won.

The following year she entered a clay court tournament, where she beat the world's best player, Margaret Court, in the semi-final. Her first Grand Slam entry came in the US Open in 1971. She staged three remarkable comebacks and only lost to Billie Jean King in the semi-final, her first defeat after a 46-match winning streak. She was clearly developing into a force to be reckoned with on the women's tour.

Martina Navratilova's upbringing was markedly different and was filled with adversity from an early age that would have broken most children. She was born in Prague in 1956, but her parents divorced when she was three. Her father Mirek remarried but committed suicide when she was just eight. Her mother also remarried and her new husband, Miroslav Navratil, became the young Martina's first coach. Her grandparents also played so the sport was clearly in the blood.

Aged only 15, Navratilova won the 1972 national tennis championships. (Some say she was inspired by a picture of Evert on the wall of her tennis club in the tiny village of Revnice just outside Prague.) She made her debut on the US Lawn Tennis Association tour the following year but she didn't turn professional until 1975. She reached the finals of both the Australian Open and the French Open in her first pro year, losing the latter to Chris Evert. Later in the same year she again lost to Evert, this time in the semi-final of the US Open. After the match she visited the Immigration and Naturalisation Service saying she wished to defect from her home country. She received her green card within a few weeks and the stage was set for nearly a generation of great matches between the pair.

Navratilova recorded her first win over Evert in a tense quarter-final in Washington later the same year, but Evert still didn't feel Navratilova would give her much of a challenge in the long run as she was nearly two stone overweight. The two met in the final of the Virginia Slims tournament in Houston in 1976, with Evert having won their previous six finals. By now Navratilova had lost all the weight she'd gained after arriving in America and living on hamburgers, and she'd spent a lot of time working on her conditioning in the gym. The effort paid off and she won in straight sets. Evert needed to stand up and take notice and begrudgingly conceded defeat: "If she keeps this up, she could be pretty good."

Billie Jean King agreed. She'd had an eye on Navratilova for a couple of seasons and, while they were sharing a car between tournaments, told her that she could be the greatest player of all time if she adopted new training techniques and cut out the bad habits. Navratilova thought she was joking and dismissed the compliment.

Evert was the superstar of women's tennis, and the first to crossover into mainstream entertainment. She was hounded by the paparazzi, her love life, especially her relationship with tennis bad boy Jimmy Connors, was scrutinised by the media, and she was in demand for all the major talk shows.

Navratilova, on the other hand, was busy championing gay rights and was about to revolutionise the way players would train. But she was quick to acknowledge the contribution of the former champion: "Billie Jean made us athletes. Chris made us celebrities."

By now Evert was keeping a close eye on her rival's results and, after watching Navratilova beat Margaret Court, Virginia Wade and Evonne Goolagong in quick succession, decided to ask the former Czech to be her doubles partner. Navratilova was flattered and accepted immediately and the pair's friendship grew stronger by the tournament. Evert was still the dominant partner, however, and was undoubtedly the best player in the world between 1973 and 1977, claiming the French Open in 1974 and 1975, Wimbledon in 1974 and the US Open from 1975 to 1978.

Evert's tumultuous personal life and a couple of high-profile defeats prompted her to take a sabbatical in late 1977. She was tired of the press intrusion and had just lost a Wimbledon semifinal to eventual champion Virginia Wade. She refused to do the post-match interview and ended up sobbing in the dressing room, before trashing her hotel room a little later. With Navratilova still not at her peak, the tennis world thought it was being deprived of a Goolagong-Evert rivalry, but the Australian had settled into married life and only concentrated on her home Grand Slam.

By 1978 Evert was ready to return, but by then Navratilova was a vastly different proposition. Her first 36 tournaments had yielded just two victories, compared with Evert's 36 wins from only 49 events, but the balance of power was finally moving across the net.

Evert believed Navratilova was gradually working her out after all the time they'd spent on the practise court together, so she dissolved their doubles partnership. Navratilova concedes that this may be partly true, but she was also seeking advice on how to deal with the psychological aspects of her game from partner Sandra Haynie, a Major golf winner who coached her how to deal with defeat, speak to the press, control her diet and rein in her emotions during matches.

This role was continued by professional basketball player and WNBA coach Nancy Lieberman in the early 1980s. She encouraged Navratilova to train until she broke down in pain, the sole aim of this agony being to kill Chrissie on the court. The change in Navratilova's form and fortune was immediate and she emerged from a lacklustre period in her career lean and focused. Evert had won 25 of their first 33 encounters, from their initial meeting at the Akron Indoors tournament in 1973 to their Wimbledon warm-up at Eastbourne in 1979. From then on, however, the tide turned in Navratilova's favour. She won 10 of their next 14 matches before Evert won the final of the 1982 Australian Open. She then enjoyed a long period of dominance over Evert, winning 25 of their last 33 matches, including 13 in a row between 1982 and 1984.

If a single turning point in the rivalry could be picked, Navratilova cites the 1978 Wimbledon final. Both players were clearly nervous, although Evert seemed to handle the pressure better and took the first set comfortably (6-2) after Navratilova played an extraordinary air shot while trying a simple overhead, and then took a ball in the back of the head in the same game. The players laughed off an incident that only seemed to spur Navratilova on. Her plan to storm the net appeared not to be working initially, but she was now crowding Evert and the relentless pressure began to tell. She soon started reaching Evert's defensive lobs and putting them away.

After a number of hard-hitting rallies, Navratilova took the second set 6-4. Although Evert was still favourite to hold on for outright victory, she began to falter at the beginning of the decisive set. Navratilova raced into a two-game lead, but Evert somehow managed to claw her way back into the match and took four straight games. Now it was Navratilova's turn to fight for every point and she won 12 of the next 13 to take the title (2-6, 6-4, 7-5) and the coveted world number one spot for the first time, her pinpoint volleying and tracer-like returns proving too much for a tiring Evert, whose game had disintegrated.

Navratilova was still viewed by some experts as mentally fragile and tactically naïve, so she hired transsexual coach Renee Richards to fine-tune her game. Richards was an inspired choice: she insisted Navratilova watch all her opponents' matches before ironing out her own faults and developing strategies to beat them. She changed from the person who could be a set and a break up but who still feared she might choke to the woman who looked across the net at her opponent and knew she would win inside 45 minutes. It was an incredible emotional turnaround.

Navratilova then spent the entire 1981 US Open preparing for a semi-final showdown with Evert. Six months earlier Evert had embarrassed her 6-0, 6-0 and the critics were saying Navratilova was a spent force who would never realise her potential. Navratilova proved the doubters wrong with a blistering serve-volley display to win in three sets. She then emphasised her new-found belief by beating Evert again in the Australian Open final.

It was during the lean years that followed that Evert enjoyed perhaps her finest on-court moment. She'd previously joked that Martina should go and join the men's tour to give everyone else a chance, and no one gave her a hope of beating her great rival in the final of the 1985 French Open because Navratilova had only lost eight matches out of her previous 300 over the last three seasons. But Evert had begun to realise that all the top athletes were changing their diet and incorporating weightlifting programmes into their training sessions. She knew this would complement her flawless ground-strokes and perfect technique and it was the only way to revive her game against an opponent who was forging ahead in their personal battle. And Evert was a clay court specialist who'd already won the French Open title five times.

After a keenly contested match, during which she lost a second-set tie-break, Evert finally passed Navratilova down the line with a pinpoint backhand to take the title. It was the shot of a lifetime, one that every professional dreams about, and the crowd at Roland Garros gave her a thunderous ovation. The win almost certainly rekindled her interest in the sport and she delayed her retirement by another four years.

Although Navratilova gave the impression of being dour, serious and incredibly difficult to be beat, both women agree that, of the two, she was actually the more emotional. When they played, Evert, the Ice Maiden, was usually the steelier opponent. To the public they were polar opposites – Evert the pin-up, wholesome girl next door who played elegantly from the base-line, Navratilova the aggressive Eastern Bloc machine who played serve-volley – but the reality is they shared many common bonds. Indeed, while Evert seemed to be able to maintain her composure, Navratilova often let her emotions come flooding out.

On the practise court their roles were often reversed. Evert would swear and break racquets, while Navratilova would calmly analyse her faults and correct them. Evert's father managed to talk her out of showing this kind of emotion on court because he believed it would give her opponents an advantage.

Navratilova always felt that, once she was in the ascendancy, she was seen by the public as the villain of the piece, the muscular foreign lesbian. Evert, the all-American girl, simply couldn't be beaten by the defector from a communist state. Indeed, when Evert was introduced to the crowd before

87

several of their finals everyone clapped, but when Navratilova's name was announced only a smattering of applause circled the arena. Only later on in their careers was Navratilova finally accepted by the American public.

Statistics often don't tell the full story, but there are some impressive numbers when discussing the Evert-Navratilova rivalry. Evert won 157 singles titles to Navratilova's record 167. Evert won 125 consecutive matches on clay; Navratilova won 74 straight singles matches on all surfaces and 109 consecutive doubles matches with Pam Shriver, both of which are outright records. Evert reached the semi-finals in 52 of the 56 Grand Slams she entered between 1971 and 1989. Between 1982 and 1986 they won 18 of the 20 Grand Slam singles titles on offer and they exchanged the world number one spot 17 times over a period of 12 years.

The pair met 14 times in Grand Slam finals, with Navratilova winning 10. Of the 80 matches they played overall, she edges Evert out 43-37. By the time she retired in 1989, Evert had clocked up 1309 singles victories with only 146 defeats. This 90 per cent success rate is unequalled in the history of professional tennis, by man or woman. Navratilova carried on until 2006 when, at the age of 49, she took the mixed doubles title at the US Open with Bob Bryan.

"There's a closeness that Chris and I share that we won't ever have with anyone else. It doesn't matter if we don't see each other for a week or a year because it's like we just saw each other yesterday. I'm so happy to have been one half of that whole." Martina Navratilova

"She was part of my life every day for thirty years. And the respect and admiration were always there." Chris Evert

Both were fiercely independent and ambitious to the point of cutting out partners and loved ones if they encroached on their careers. Indeed Evert is quick to blame herself, at least in part, for the way her marriage to John Lloyd suffered in the early 1980s, while Navratilova found herself ostracised by her father when she told him she was gay. But without their sheer determination, skill and longevity they would not be considered alongside the best athletes the sporting world has ever seen.

Together they helped reshape the culture of women's sport, and, by changing the way tennis was played and raising the standard to a level that had not previously been achieved, Evert and Navratilova will always be mentioned in the same breath and will be remembered for as long as the game itself.

Verdict: There's no doubt that Evert had the upper hand in their early meetings, and she remained the dominant force on clay throughout their careers, but Navratilova took control during the middle years of their rivalry and never relinquished that advantage. Her nine Wimbledon titles help her take the contest by a whisker.

Bobby Fischer

vs

Russia, Boris Spassky and himself

Child prodigy. Genius. The King of Chess. Bobby Fischer, who died aged 64 in January 2008, had many monikers attached to him throughout his chequered life, but there is absolutely no doubt that this enigmatic, often difficult and complex character, changed the face and the image of the game of chess forever.

At his best, no one could touch him, and few ever came close. But this is not to say he didn't enjoy a rivalry that kept pushing him to new heights. The early 1970s may not have been the height of the Cold War, but the atmosphere between the two superpowers was still icy. And so it was, when, in 1972, Fischer took part in his most celebrated match, against the Russian grandmaster Boris Spassky.

This encounter, which gripped television audiences around the world, was the ultimate sporting metaphor and came to be seen as a symbol of Cold War rivalry.

For the USSR, chess had always been a key weapon in the Cold War. Even more than sport, the cerebral character of chess gave it added significance in asserting Soviet superiority over the West. And in Spassky, the sport possessed the most charming, good-looking and popular of all Soviet world champions.

But America had Fischer. His guile on the chessboard and his electric charisma off it sparked a rivalry unlike any other in this book, one against an entire nation. Tall and striking, Fischer provided the game with that rare commodity: star quality. He turned up late for tournaments, walked out of matches, refused to play unless the lighting suited him and didn't tolerate photographers and cartoonists.

He was the game's first star, and to this day, if you ask anyone to name one chess player, the two names that crop up most will be Garry Kasparov and Bobby Fischer.

However, contrary to popular belief, Fischer did not emerge from the womb a full-blown grandmaster. Born in Chicago and raised in Brooklyn, as a child he was essentially a hotshot club player – a prodigy, for certain, but not someone who was potential world-championship material.

But in 1956, at the age of 13, Fischer made a colossal leap. That year he became the youngest player ever to win the US Junior Championship. He also dominated the US tournament circuit. What was astounding wasn't simply that a gawky 13-year-old kid in blue jeans was suddenly winning tournaments. It was the way he was winning. He didn't just beat people – he humiliated them.

The thing he relished most was making his opponents as uncomfortable as possible. "I like the moment when I break a man's ego," he once said. Later in the year he played a game so remarkable that it was immediately dubbed 'The Game of the Century'.

Fischer faced Donald Byrne, then one of the top 10 US players, in New York. The battle was jam-packed with complex combinations, ingenious sacrifices, danger and apparent danger – enough to make Fischer, who won, a chess god overnight. Asked to explain his sudden emergence on the world stage, he shrugged and said: "I just got good."

The duel was dissected in newspapers and magazines around the world and won Fischer the Brilliancy Prize, an annual chess award that recognises particularly imaginative play. Even the Russians, loath to acknowledge so much as the existence of American players, grudgingly tipped their hats. Mikhail Botvinnik, the reigning world champion, reportedly said: "We will have to start keeping an eye on this boy."

That is exactly what the chess world did from that moment on. Fischer's achievements were staggering: in his time he was the youngest US master (at 14 years and five months), the youngest international grandmaster, and the youngest candidate for the world championship (at 15 years and six months). He also won eight US chess championship titles – a record not likely to be broken.

In 1966 he co-authored *Bobby Fischer Teaches Chess*, the bestselling chess book ever written, and in 1969 he published *My 60 Memorable Games*, arguably the best chess book.

Fischer also won a lot of games – an impressive fact given that draws among grandmasters are commonplace. At the highest level, players are so familiar with one another's games that they can practically read their opponents' minds.

But Fischer didn't play for draws. Like the greatest of them all, Muhammad Ali, he was always on the attack – even rhetorically. Of the Soviet champions who had dominated the game so completely, he said: "They have nothing on me, those guys. They can't even touch me."

The Soviets were not amused. They dismissed the young American upstart as *nyekulturni* – literally, 'uncultured'. This wasn't far from the truth, and Fischer knew it. He lacked education, and had always been insecure about this. His deficiency was particularly glaring now that most of his interaction was with adults, many of them sophisticated and well-read.

In the autumn of 1968 Fischer walked out of the Chess Olympiad in Switzerland. He refused to play for another 18 months, and some feared that his competitive drive had stalled, but that wasn't the case.

He was still training 14 hours a day and playing chess privately. In 1970 he returned to public competition and had the longest winning streak in tournament chess: 20 consecutive outright victories against the world's top grandmasters. And so it was that by 1972 Fischer had reached his peak.

The world champion, Boris Spassky, agreed to meet him in Reykjavik to play what would be the most carefully scrutinised match.

For Fischer the showdown pitted "the free world against the lying, cheating, hypocritical Russians". Inevitably, the match became a Cold War battleground. Richard Nixon sent Fisher his personal congratulations and assured him that "I will be rooting for you." Secretary of State Henry Kissinger also put in a call: "America wants you to go over there to beat the Russians."

However, although Fischer had worked his entire life for an opportunity to play for the world crown, now that he finally had the chance, he began to be overtaken by anxiety, self-doubt, and paranoia (he feared the Soviets would shoot down his plane).

All the youthful bravado and swagger – the bum-of-the-month club, the taunting of the Russians – were distant memories. There were rumours that state officials had to drag Bobby kicking and screaming to play in Iceland.

The prize money troubled Fischer too. When Spassky won the title in 1969 his take was a paltry $1,400. The promoters in Iceland were willing to pump the prize money up, but not to a level Fischer deemed sufficient. When a handsome five-figure purse was suggested, Fischer threatened a no-show. When Spassky and his entourage arrived in Reykjavik, a grumbling Fischer was still in New York.

After a series of escalating demands, Fischer managed to drive up the prize money to $250,000 and he was guaranteed a considerable slice of film or TV revenues. But even then the match hit a snag. Fischer refused to play because his favourite television programme, *The Jack LaLanne Show*, wasn't available on Icelandic TV. It was Lina Grumette, a Los Angeles chess promoter and Fischer's 'chess mother' at the time, who finally managed to talk him into playing.

Finally, the high school dropout, armed with little more than a pocket chess set and a dog-eared book documenting Spassky's important games, was ready. And his performance in Iceland was no disappointment. He put on a show that was equal parts soap opera and political thriller. And between acts he managed to play some brilliant chess.

The games were an instant hit. Chess pundit Shelby Lyman's *World Chess Championship* was at the time the highest-rated PBS show ever – a feat that was all the more amazing given that it consisted of little more than a giant wall-

93

mounted chess board on which each move was recorded and discussed by analysts.

Fischer played poorly in the opening match on July 12th and Spassky won easily. Fischer refused to play the second game unless all cameras were removed from the hall. The organisers tried to minimise their intrusiveness but he still refused to play.

Finally, Fischer was warned that if his demands didn't stop, game two would be awarded to Spassky. Fischer thought, wrongly, that they were bluffing and ended up forfeiting the game. Suddenly he was in a hole, with Spassky ahead by two games to nil. To placate Fischer, the third game was played in another room and broadcast to the dismayed audience on closed-circuit television. He won handily.

The players then returned to the exhibition hall, and Fischer soon grabbed the lead and held it, albeit still complaining about the cameras (in the end only a small amount of the match was filmed), the surface of the chess board (too shiny), the proximity of the audience (he insisted the first seven rows of seats be removed), and the ambient noise.

Members of the Soviet delegation began to make their own unreasonable demands, hoping to unnerve Fischer. They accused him of using a concealed device to interfere with Spassky's brain waves. The match was halted while police officers searched the playing hall. Fischer's chair was taken apart, light fixtures were dismantled, and the entire auditorium was swept for suspicious electronic signals. Nothing was found.

Fischer wasn't flustered. If anything, his play became stronger. As the weeks wore on, Spassky slowly began to crack, and on September 1st, with Fischer leading 11-8, the Russian resigned, thus losing game 21, the match and the title.

A brash 29-year-old had single-handedly defeated the Soviet chess juggernaut. Spassky had a wealth of resources at his disposal to help him plot moves, including 35 grandmasters back in the Soviet Union. Dutch grandmaster Jan Timman called Fischer's victory "the story of a lonely hero who overcomes an entire empire".

The effect that Fischer had on the game back in his homeland was instantaneous, not to mention immense. A 'Fischer Boom' saw membership in the US Chess Federation double in 1972 and peak in 1974.

Unfortunately for the sport, the mysterious and paranoid Fischer never defended his title. He was scheduled to defend it in 1975 against Anatoly Karpov, but only after making three specific demands to the International Chess Federation. Two of his demands were rejected so he refused to play Karpov, meaning the Russian became world champion by default.

In his autobiography, Karpov expressed profound regret that the match did not take place, and claimed that the lost opportunity to challenge Fischer held back his own chess development. Karpov met Fischer several times after 1975, in friendly but ultimately unsuccessful attempts to arrange a match.

After losing his title, Fischer dropped out of competitive chess and largely out of view, living in Hungary, the Philippines and Japan. He later renounced his US citizenship and settled in Iceland.

However, after twenty years, Fischer emerged from isolation to play Spassky (then tied for 96th-102nd on the FIDE rating list) in Belgrade in 1992 in what was billed as the 'Revenge Match of the 20th Century'.

Fischer demanded that the organisers also bill the match as The World Chess Championship, although Garry Kasparov was the recognised world champion. Fischer insisted he was still the true world champion however, and the purse for his rematch with Spassky was US$5,000,000, with $3.35 million of that going to the winner.

Fischer won the match, 10 wins to 5 losses with 15 draws. He never played any competitive games afterwards and returned to obscurity.

He emerged occasionally from his life as a recluse to say something outrageous and usually offensive. His fragile mental health led to poisonous and very public outbursts – especially after 9/11 – that prompted global revulsion. Fischer praised the terrorist attacks, saying that he wanted "to see the US wiped out".

In his last years, Fischer directed his venom at the chess establishment, alleging that the outcomes of many top-level matches were decided in advance.

Then, on January 17th 2008, Fischer died in Reykjavík after

a long illness for which he had refused treatment. Even this was somehow typical of Fischer, who grew up playing chess against himself since he had no one else to play. He had fought to the end and proven himself to be his most dangerous opponent.

Bobby Fischer was one of a kind, the chess world's flawed genius. His mercurial brilliance was undisputed and his relentless, even pathological dedication transformed the world of chess. His accomplishment in the sport cannot be overstated, and his legacy may never be matched. In the words of one Russian grandmaster, he was "an Achilles without an Achilles heel".

The verdict: Despite his controversial and sometimes insulting persona, Fischer is the winner. He revolutionised the game, although by refusing to defend his title no one will ever know how great he could have become.

Larry Bird

vs

Magic Johnson

Right from the beginning, the careers of Larry Bird and Magic Johnson were inexorably headed down the same path.

An icon in Boston Celtic green, Larry Bird hailed from a small town called French Lick in Indiana. A player of boundless determination, Bird's unremitting focus, dynamite jump shot and constant demand for excellence from his team-mates left opponents quaking.

On the other side, resplendent in purple and gold, you had a magician with a magnetic personality by the name of Earvin Johnson. Take a bow, Mr Showtime, a man with an equally inextinguishable desire to win and a natural talent that led him to the one nickname that could do him justice: Magic.

They played each other for the national college championships; they both turned professional in the same year. Bird was East Coast; Magic the West. Their unequalled competitive relationship came to symbolise the most thrilling rivalry in the history of the NBA. Billy Wilder couldn't have written a better script.

Earvin 'Magic' Johnson grew up outside Detroit in Lansing, Michigan, one of seven children. His family had moved up from the South in the 1950s to look for jobs in the auto plants. Johnson's father worked the assembly line night shift at General Motors and, to bring in some extra cash, he started a trash hauling business on the side.

Johnson was a happy, joke-making boy who loved two things: garnering attention and playing basketball. He focused on the game from an early age, hitting the local court at six in the morning to get in some practise before elementary school.

Later on, Johnson took a bus to a majority-white high school, where racial tensions ran high – blacks and whites simply did not associate with one another, except to fight. But Johnson's easygoing demeanour and basketball skills made him a bridge between the warring factions and the principal often asked him to play peacemaker.

Though Johnson could have taken his pick of college scholarships, he decided to stay at home and attend Michigan State, where he developed into a player of supreme talent, not to mention astonishing versatility.

Johnson was exceptional because he played point guard despite being 6'9", a size normally reserved for front-court players. He combined the size of a power forward, the one-on-one skills of a swingman (a player who could play both the small forward and shooting guard role), and the ball handling talent of a guard, making him a dangerous triple threat.

Larry Bird grew up less than 400 miles away in tiny, rural French Lick, Indiana. He was one of six kids in a poor family that was below Johnson's on the economic scale. Bird's mother worked as a waitress and a cook, while his father, a Korean War veteran, took odd jobs but was often out of work.

A withdrawn, shy kid, Bird found an outlet in basketball. At 13, he visited his aunt in another part of Indiana, got in a pickup game and dominated. The other kids on his team slapped him on the back, told him he was great and asked Bird to keep playing with them. Bird later called it "the day I fell in love with basketball".

Like Magic, Bird became a heavily courted high school basketball star. He took a scholarship to play for Bobby Knight at Indiana, but found the adjustment from rural poverty to university jarring.

After only 24 days, he dropped out and hitchhiked home. When he arrived back in French Lick, his mother refused to speak to him for months.

Bird took a job with the municipality, cutting grass, painting park benches and driving a garbage truck. He also played AAU basketball, destroying competition across Indiana. The next year, Bird returned to college at Indiana State University, 75 miles away in Terre Haute, where he found the atmosphere suited him better.

Michigan State and Indiana State were not college basketball powerhouses. But Magic and Bird immediately energised the fortunes of both colleges, a feat they would later achieve in the NBA.

In his freshman year, Johnson took a team that had been 10-17 the previous season and led it to a 25-5 record, its first Big Ten championship in two decades and the Elite Eight.

Indiana State had been 12-14 in the two seasons before Bird arrived. For the three years he played there – he had to sit out his first year due to NCAA rules – ISU went 81-13.

In 1979 – the end of Johnson's second year playing for Michigan State and Bird's third at Indiana State – the pair led their teams to the NCAA championship game. Michigan State won 75-64.

By that time, Bird and Johnson had become national stories, phenomena that had seemingly come from nowhere. The game remains the highest-rated in college basketball history. Johnson was voted Final Four MVP. Bird, who was the College Player of the Year, had a poor game, and the loss still gnaws at him to this day. "It's the one thing I'll never get over," he has said.

Both players' NBA careers hit the ground running. Johnson was more than living up to his Magic moniker, winning the NBA title against the Philadelphia 76ers in his rookie season in 1980, capping it off by filling in for the injured Kareem Abdul-Jabbar at centre and scoring 42 points to shock the 76ers in game six of the Finals. He was also awarded the Finals MVP, the first (and last) rookie to achieve this.

However, Bird's Celtics wasted no time in showing the Lakers that they could emulate their success. They captured the NBA title in 1981, defeating the Houston Rockets, and the Celtics' new man was at the forefront of their success.

His talent for recognising the moves of opponents and teammates prompted Bill Fitch, his first coach with the Celtics, to give him the nickname 'Kodak', because he seemed to formulate mental pictures of every play that took place on the court.

But Bird's first title would be eclipsed by Magic's second when the dazzling Lakers wrested the crown back at the first attempt in 1982.

Their rivalry was gripping everyone within the sport; the league had essentially become Bird, Magic and a few hundred supporting players. Their intense rivalry rejuvenated the fortunes of the ailing league and their ascendancy coincided with cable television overtaking the sports market in the US.

In 1979, the league's four-year deal with CBS was worth $74 million. By 2002 the league had signed a six-year deal with ABC, ESPN and TNT valued at $4.6 billion.

The two most popular jerseys with the fans in the mid-eighties were Magic's number 32 and Larry's number 33. In 1984, the NBA's retail merchandise generated $44 million. By 2007, that had jumped to an eye-watering $3 billion, such is the effect that these men had.

Everything had become possible because of these two players; they had captured the imagination of the entire basketball world. Their team-orientated ethos combined with a sixth sense that raised the games of their team-mates ensured the standard of basketball in the NBA had never been higher.

The one thing everyone wanted however was for them to face each other for the ultimate crown on the ultimate stage. This wish was eventually granted in 1984 when the Celtics met the Lakers in the NBA Finals.

It was Bird who soared highest in the series, averaging 27.4 points and 14 rebounds per game, earning him the coveted award of Finals' Most Valuable Player for the first time. Bird was also named the league's regular season MVP for that year.

But the following campaign was what Johnson himself called the greatest in his career. The two teams faced each other once more and this time, assisted by the legendary Kareem Abdul-Jabbar, Magic led the Lakers to the crown in six games, also winning the Finals' MVP award.

In 1986, the Celtics reached the Finals again, where they once more faced the Houston Rockets. The imperious Celtics swept the Rockets aside in six games and Bird deservedly walked away with the MVP for the third and final time in his career.

The Lakers and Celtics would meet again in 1987. But the Celtics were ravaged by injury and lost in six memorable encounters to a dominant Lakers team, inspired, of course, by Johnson. And it was Johnson's graceful, arching sky hook in game four at the Boston Garden that defined the series, ushering in a one-point victory for the away side when all hope looked lost.

After the game Bird saluted Magic as "the best I have ever seen"; Magic, gracious as ever, was unequivocal in his belief that "there's only one Larry Bird".

Unfortunately, after this epic series, the years began to catch up with them, and a new superstar in the form of Michael Jordan and the erosion of Bird and Magic's physical abilities contributed to their gradual decline.

For the last six years of his career, until his retirement in 1992, Bird was increasingly hampered by a bad back, and his beloved Celtics never made it back to the Finals after their defeat against the Lakers in 1987.

Magic, in the meantime, led the Lakers to a repeat championship in 1988, defeating Isiah Thomas's Detroit Pistons. However, the next year, in the same match-up, the Lakers lost in four games. The Lakers made it to the Finals again in 1991 but fell 4-1 to Jordan and Scottie Pippen's ascendant Chicago Bulls.

But then, in November 1991, the basketball world was hit with a revelation that silenced and shocked everyone within the sport: Magic told the world that he had contracted HIV and was immediately retiring from the NBA.

Despite his retirement, Johnson was voted by fans as a starter for the 1992 NBA All-Star Game at Orlando Arena. In true Hollywood fashion, Johnson led the West to a 153–113 win and was crowned All-Star MVP. The game ended after he made a last-minute three-pointer, and players from both teams ran onto the court to congratulate Johnson.

In 1992, Bird and Magic united for a celebratory bow as part of the Olympic Dream Team in Barcelona, joining Jordan, Pippen, Charles Barkley, Patrick Ewing and a host of other NBA superstars. It was the greatest basketball team ever assembled and unsurprisingly they annihilated their opposition, cruising to victory by an average of 45.8 points and securing the gold medal by beating Croatia 117-85 in the final.

But within a year, and with the Dream Team's Olympic victory still intoxicating him, Magic decided the lure of the game he loved was too much. He wanted to return.

Once word circulated that he was coming back long term, the goodwill toward him began to diminish. Despite the measures taken by the NBA to protect its players, many within the game were ignorant of the effects of the virus and they didn't know how to handle the news.

Players were frightened and his peers began to question whether he should return. As a result, the pressure for the game's commissioner, David Stern, to ban Magic from playing increased dramatically.

But Stern stoically stood his ground. However, not long after the announcement, the Lakers were playing the Cleveland Cavaliers when Magic was scratched on his arm. The reaction of some of the players and the collective gasp from the fans dismayed Johnson. He could see the fear and concern and knew immediately that he could no longer play the game he loved. Devastated by the criticism, he retired on the spot.

He did, however, make a brief comeback five years later. After reaching the first round of the playoffs, which ended in defeat against Houston, Magic announced his final retirement, satisfied in the knowledge that this time he had ended his career on his terms, not someone else's.

Together, Magic and Larry amassed 39,498 career points, 15,533 rebounds and 3,280 steals. However, these numbers don't begin to explain their impact on the game. When they both decided to retire, you could almost sense the NBA letting out a collective sigh.

While Michael Jordan is widely regarded as the best player of his generation, he never had a consistent foil to measure himself against. He was a singular sensation, while Magic and Larry were brilliance in tandem.

Plus, Jordan never brought the other players to a different level in the way that Bird and Magic did. Everyone who watched and loved the sport savoured every game they played. Their unselfish style of play and natural instinct for when to shoot and when to pass permeated those around them, lifting those lesser mortals to a higher plane.

Their college rivalry pulled an audience toward the NBA that otherwise might never have come, and their careers in a league that represents the zenith of world basketball rejuvenated an ailing institution.

Each pushed the other to greatness. Together they won eight NBA Championships (three for Bird, five for Magic) and six MVP awards (three each). They started as bitter rivals, but ended up lifelong friends.

Today, the Celtics/Lakers rivalry that defines the history of the NBA is undiminished, and while the new crowd favourites are the likes of Bryant and Garnett, they will never be held in the same affection as the two names forever linked with these iconic teams. Their titanic rivalry is one for the ages; they are tied to their respective teams forever and to one another.

When the game belonged to them they shared a bond forged by intense competition, and today their friendship burns as brightly as their on-court legacy. Magic and Larry, the greatest American sporting rivalry since Frazier and Ali.

Verdict: Stalemate. Their achievements are too intertwined, their effect on the game they loved and graced so magnificently too significant to separate them.

Bobby Fischer contemplates his next move

A concession during the epic
Fischer-Spassky Cold War tussle

Fischer vs Spassky in 1972

Magic vs Bird - utter determination

Larry and Magic united in admiration at Bird's retirement

The famous concession from Nicklaus
to Jacklin at the 1969 Ryder Cup

The Matador – Seve Ballesteros – the man who
made Europe the Ryder Cup force they are today

Europe's team captain José-María Olazábal celebrates
retaining the famous trophy at Medinah in 2012

Daley Thompson powers ahead of great
rival Jürgen Hingsen in the 110m hurdles

Hingsen lines up for the 100 metres
at the 1984 Olympic Games

Thompson stands like a sporting colossus amongst rivals who are exhausted after the 1500m. He later said he would have collapsed too but there was no room to lie down!

Thompson whistles the national anthem having beaten Hingsen at the 1984 Los Angeles Olympics

Frazier floors Ali with his trademark left hook in
the final round of the Fight of the Century at
Madison Square Garden in 1971

The epic final contest between the two:
The Thriller in Manila in 1975

Ronald Koeman wipes his backside
with Olaf Thon's jersey and almost
sparks a riot amongst the fans

Frank Rijkaard and Rudi Völler come to blows at Italia '90

Völler then finds time to wind up Dutch goalkeeper
Hans van Breukelen

Jürgen Klinsmann appearing to be shot
by a Dutch sniper

Alain Prost and Ayrton Senna meet for the first
time, at the opening of the new Nürburgring in
1984. In identical cars, Senna beat Prost and a
host of former F1 World Champions

Alain Prost at the 1985 German Grand Prix
driving a McLaren

Suzuka in Japan provides the backdrop for a collision
between the pair. This accident decided the 1989 title
in Prost's favour

The moment of impact between Senna and Prost at
Suzuka that decided the 1990 World Championship,
this time in Senna's favour

The Ryder Cup

In the recent Ryder Cup in Chicago, which ended in the most dramatic fashion, one fact more than any other was apparent: this tournament is the finest that golf has to offer.

A plethora of factors vindicate this. The sheer bedlam and emotion you see from the galleries, encapsulated in the massive roars that ring out around the course every time a significant putt is holed or fairway found. Then there's the pervading feeling that this competition is of utmost importance, that it really matters to players and fans. And then you have the 'us versus them' factor – the difficult-to-quantify ingredient that establishes the Ryder Cup as two rivals competing for supremacy, with both desperate for success.

However, it wasn't always this way. A sense of rivalry was barely apparent in the decades that led up to the groundbreaking decision in 1979 to include the rest of Europe in the mix. To appreciate the magnitude of this decision, you have to go back to the event's inception.

The Ryder Cup began in somewhat humble circumstances, the pipedream of a St Albans' seed merchant. Following a Ryder Cup-style exhibition match at Gleneagles in 1921 between a team of American professionals and a side drawn from the British PGA, a second was scheduled for 1926 at Surrey's East Course at Wentworth.

Great Britain won both of these contests convincingly, but it was at the second match that Samuel Ryder, having been captivated by some of the world's best players, thought it would be a good idea to make the match official. Thus the Ryder Cup was founded and the first competition proper took place in 1927 at Worcester Country Club in Massachusetts, with Ryder donating the trophy.

Early matches between the two sides were fairly even but, after the Second World War, the Americans began to dominate. They would go on to win 18 out of the following 22 events, occasionally punctuated by a courageous British performance (such as the legendary 'Concession' at Royal Birkdale in 1969).

It was so one-sided, in fact, that for some American players there was little point in playing as the event didn't showcase their skills. The 1973 Open champion Tom Weiskopf, for instance, decided not to play at Royal Lytham & St Annes in 1977, taking the opportunity to go bear-hunting in Alaska instead. The antipathy of players such as Weiskopf typified a wider indifference, especially in America.

It was obvious that due to the one-sided nature of the event the Ryder Cup was losing its appeal. In fact, many questioned whether the competition had a future. With humiliation heaped on humiliation and an absence of anything resembling a contest, the television companies had all but lost interest. Tough decisions had to be made...and quickly. The Ryder Cup had long since ceased to be a genuine contest.

The decision to include continental Europeans arose from a discussion in 1977 between Jack Nicklaus and the Earl of Derby, who was serving as the President of the Professional Golfers' Association. This radical measure was suggested by Nicklaus as a means to make the matches more competitive, to make the predictable nature of the event a thing of the past.

Unfortunately, decades of ugly, landslide defeats for the British team had left the side dispirited, the opposition indifferent and the future of the event hanging in the balance. Even when a desperate and despairing Professional Golf Association (PGA) widened its selection pool, first from Great Britain to Great Britain & Ireland and then to a Europe-wide team, it seemed, initially at least, to make little difference.

In the new European team's first outing at West Virginia's The Greenbrier in 1979, they were hammered 17-11, and worse was to follow. Two years later, at Walton Heath, the Americans brought arguably the greatest Ryder Cup side ever assembled across the Atlantic and demolished them once again, 18½-9½.

The inescapable truth was that the decision to bring the Europeans into the fray hadn't had the immediate effect that Nicklaus et al desired. To stop the event from finally being put out of its misery, the European PGA needed to do something dramatic to save it from becoming a forgotten relic.

When the PGA asked one of Europe's most successful players, double Major winner Tony Jacklin, to skipper the team for the 1983 tournament in Florida, there were just six months before it began. Moreover, there wasn't exactly a queue of candidates for the job.

Jacklin would agree to the job, but only if a raft of assurances could be guaranteed. From team rooms and support staff to better clothing and new equipment, plus travel on Concorde for wives and the caddies, too. "I said, if I do it, it has got to be the way the Americans do it," Jacklin proclaimed.

Thanks to Jacklin, the European team now looked – and felt – better than ever, and his positive approach didn't stop there: Jacklin's team selection indicated he meant business too. A revitalised Seve Ballesteros was back following his omission in 1981, and he was inspired by a stirring war-cry from his skipper. The Europeans weren't going to Palm Beach to make up the numbers; they were going with pride and belief.

This sense of determination filtered into the players' form in Florida. After the opening day, the visitors led for the first time on American soil. Both teams were level at 8-8 after the second day and, as the match progressed into the singles, an almighty battle ensued.

Ballesteros was involved in a thrilling contest with Fuzzy Zoeller and the Spaniard looked invincible at three-up with seven to play, but then his game wobbled alarmingly. He rallied at the 16th but still needed to win the final hole to take the match. Sitting in a bunker 240 yards from the pin, defeat seemed inevitable, but Ballesteros hit a three wood close to the green and got down in two to grab a remarkable half.

A miraculous pitch from Lanny Wadkins on the final hole against José Maria Cañizares gave the American a half, which ensured they retained the cup.

When future captain Bernard Gallacher failed to get anything from his singles match with Tom Watson, the hosts celebrated yet another victory but this time it was different. Defeat for Europe hurt, and not because it was another embarrassingly heavy loss – quite the opposite: it was agonisingly close and the Americans knew it. After decades of despair, the future finally looked promising.

But could the next Ryder Cup on European soil build on this change in fortunes and see the home team finally prise the Holy Grail from American hands? The event took place at The Belfry and the European team boasted, among others, Masters champion Bernhard Langer and Open winner Sandy Lyle, as well as Ian Woosnam and Nick Faldo.

The Americans started well on the first day, claiming three of the four foursomes with Lanny Wadkins and Raymond Floyd impressing in two wins. But on the second day, the pendulum began to swing towards the Europeans. Seve Ballesteros was in defiant mood, claiming his first two points playing alongside compatriot Manuel Pinero.

Europe seized the initiative, establishing a platform for their remarkable triumph. Craig Stadler and Curtis Strange – two-up with two to play against Bernhard Langer and Sandy Lyle – appeared certain to win their game.

Stadler, however, missed a three-foot putt on the last to hand their opponents an unlikely half, and with it the momentum in the match.

Europe went into the final day leading 9-7 and full of confidence. In the end, it was down to Sam Torrance to secure the trophy, but the Scot was facing US Open champion Andy North and had fallen three holes behind.

Torrance fought back and it was neck-and-neck going to the 18th. After North's ball found water, Torrance made birdie with an 18-foot putt. The emotional Scot, who was in tears before the putt sank, raised his arms aloft to signal that the Ryder Cup, after 28 barren years, was finally in European hands. The grand alliance between Great Britain and the rest of the continent had at last been embraced.

The European team travelled to Muirfield Village in Ohio desperate to defend their title and prove their victory at The Belfry was not a one-off. Tony Jacklin skippered Europe again and he was up against his old adversary Jack Nicklaus, rekindling the fond memories of their epic Ryder Cup tussle in 1969 – one of the rare occasions when the Great Britain team came close to winning.

That 1969 encounter, played at Royal Birkdale, ended in the Ryder Cup's first tie after perhaps the most sporting concession in golfing history. The final match saw Nicklaus level with Jacklin going up the final hole. The Golden Bear, playing in his first Ryder Cup, holed a four-foot putt to ensure America would retain the trophy.

However, rather than force Jacklin to hole a three-foot putt to halve their match, he conceded it, saying: "I don't think you would have missed that putt, but in these circumstances I would never give you the opportunity." The sporting world stood back in awe, all except US captain Sam Snead, who couldn't believe his star player had not made Jacklin putt.

At Muirfield Village 18 years later, events played out in similarly enthralling circumstances. The Europeans dominated the first two days' play and went into the final day's singles with a five-point lead. However, despite working their way into this commanding position, no one expected the final push to be easy and the Americans didn't waste time putting points on the scoreboard.

In the first match, mercurial Welsh wizard Ian Woosnam was one hole down going into the last against Andy Bean, but he could not summon up the birdie he needed for victory and the Americans were up and running. Then, Nick Faldo and José Maria Olazábal surprisingly lost against Mark Calcavecchia and Payne Stewart respectively and suddenly the tide was turning.

It was the increasingly tense game between Eamonn Darcy and Ben Crenshaw – which had exploded on the sixth green when Crenshaw, already two holes down, snapped his own putter in a fit of rage – that would help to settle the European team's nerves and send them on to victory.

Crenshaw – one of the game's greatest putters – had to complete his round putting with either a one iron or a sand wedge but, amazingly, he bounced back to all square going into the last. However, Darcy held his nerve and claimed an unlikely victory in his fourth Ryder Cup match.

And so it came down to the steely nerve of Bernhard Langer and the enigmatic brilliance of Seve to bring it home, with the safest of fours at the 17th from the Spaniard securing the cup for Europe. After a day of unbearable tension and excitement, they finally triumphed by 15 points to 13.

Following these back-to-back European victories, the hype

preceding the next event at The Belfry was immense. It was another nail-biting affair that ended in stalemate for only the second time in the tournament's history.

America had it all to do going into the final day's singles and they fought back to win the first two matches. However, their momentum soon faltered. On the treacherous 18th, Payne Stewart sent his ball into the water to lose to Olazábal, and then he could only watch in horror as team-mate Mark Calcavecchia played exactly the same shot against Ronan Rafferty.

And then came the seminal moment that will always be synonymous with the 1989 event: Christy O'Connor Junior's famous two-iron to the 18th that saw him vanquish Fred Couples. Tears were flowing on the green and off.

In the end, it fell to José Maria Cañizares to get down in two on the 18th to win his match against Ken Green and ensure that Europe retained the trophy. However, defeats in the remaining four singles matches meant that Europe could not claim overall victory.

As the Ryder Cup entered the 1990s, events in the Gulf, where America and her allies were fighting to liberate Kuwait, set the tone for a tournament that would become known as the 'War on the Shore'. This was due to the behaviour of the highly charged American players led by Corey Pavin, who proudly wore a Desert Storm cap.

Bernard Gallacher had replaced Tony Jacklin as European captain and was confident of victory, but then again, so were the Americans.

The fate of the cup was eventually decided on the last hole of the last match between Bernhard Langer and Hale Irwin. Langer, with the eyes of the world upon him, missed his six-foot putt for the half that would have given Europe a tie, and the Ryder Cup returned to America for the first time since 1983.

To quell any feelings of enmity between the sides, the Americans made the clever choice of the much-admired Tom Watson as their captain for the third consecutive event to be played at The Belfry. An amiable relationship between Watson and Gallacher developed quickly and the first two days' play ended with just one point separating the teams. It was America who triumphed, however, as they stormed to six wins and two halves in the singles.

In 1995 at Oakland Hills, Gallacher skippered the Europeans for a third time and he was determined to get his hands on the trophy. After yet more dazzling golf and another nerve-jangling finish, the Europeans snatched a dramatic victory, the unlikely figure of Philip Walton sealing it with a win against Jay Haas. After decades of effortless American superiority, Europe had secured their second victory over the pond in six years.

The trophy was heading back to Europe and it would stay there until 1999 after 1997's European victory at Valderrama. Skippered by the European team's most famous player, Seve Ballesteros, the home team amassed a commanding lead after the first two days, which proved to be just enough to withstand a last-day singles onslaught from the US team.

Going into the 1999 Ryder Cup at Brookline in Massachusetts, the home team, led by Ben Crenshaw, had grown sick of the taste of defeat. They wanted revenge and their determination to get their hands on the trophy was insatiable.

However, after the first two days the Europeans had raced into an impressive 10-6 lead. The Americans, fuelled by a pep talk from Texas governor and presidential candidate George W. Bush on the Saturday night, treated the final day like the Alamo.

Buoyed by a favourable draw and a raucous home crowd, the Americans won the first six matches of the day. Padraig Harrington pulled back a point for Europe, but the home team moved to within a half point of victory when Jim Furyk defeated Sergio Garcia.

When Justin Leonard holed a 40-foot birdie on the 17th, he looked to have sealed the comeback. Leonard ran around punching the air and was swamped by caddies, team-mates and wives. His opponent, José Maria Olazábal, who could still halve the hole with a birdie putt of his own, was left waiting on the green while the Americans celebrated presumed victory. When the pandemonium finally died down, the normally unflappable Spaniard struck his putt wide and the Americans continued their celebrations.

Their voracious march in clawing back point after point in the singles was worthy of the highest praise, but the Europeans and most of the watching world believed a line had been crossed. Sam Torrance branded the behaviour of the players and the whipped-up crowd 'disgusting', while Europe's captain, the normally placid Mark James, referred to it as a 'bear pit' in a book recounting the event

It was left to the patriotic yet calm head of Payne Stewart to put the event into perspective. "You have to understand," said Stewart in the aftermath of the unpalatable events of the Sunday afternoon, "that this is not life or death."

The distasteful end to proceedings had taken the shine off an incredible week's golf and one of the greatest comebacks in sporting history. The individual performances of the American team meant they fully deserved their triumph and the quality of their golf was at times utterly sublime.

However, for their performances as a team, the Europeans deserved more than they eventually got. Their achievement in running the opposition so close, despite being overwhelming underdogs and playing in the most hostile environment, should never be underestimated.

It was clear that time was needed for players from both sides to reflect and move on from events at Brookline. However, the next Ryder Cup, scheduled once more for The Belfry, was postponed due to the September 11 attacks. It was eventually played the following year at the original venue with the same teams that had been selected to play initially. The display boards at The Belfry still read 'The 2001 Ryder Cup'.

The sobering events of September 11 put the behaviour of the players and fans, not to mention the importance of the event, into stark context. It was clear that everyone involved in the Ryder Cup would not allow a repeat of the unsavoury atmosphere of Brookline, so, when the American team, captained by Curtis Strange, arrived in Warwickshire they were the model of respect and fair play.

After the first two days, the scores were tied at eight points each but, rather than take a cautious approach, Europe's captain, Sam Torrance, instead took a risk by sending his best players out first on the final day.

The gamble paid off handsomely. Point followed point, with Seve's successor as European talisman, Colin Montgomerie, producing arguably the greatest performance of his professional career with a 5&4 hammering of Scott Hoch.

If Monty's win was the most impressive, then the biggest surprise came in the match between Welshman Phillip Price and world number two Phil Mickelson. Price's 25-foot putt on the 16th green sealed a memorable 3&2 victory and sparked jubilant celebrations.

It was left to Paul McGinley to secure victory for Europe with a half against Jim Furyk. The Irishman celebrated by throwing himself into the lake at the 18th draped in his home flag.

Sam Torrance, so dejected and drained three years earlier, this time cut an ecstatic yet humble figure. "It had nothing to do with me," said the emotional Scot. "I led the boys to water, and they drank copiously." After three long years everyone had forgotten how good this competition could be.

Europe's comfortable 15½-12½ win was seen as a benchmark for what they could achieve, but many thought the winning margin would be difficult to emulate. However, events in 2004 at Oakland Hills confounded all expectations when Europe recorded their largest ever victory.

For many, the die was cast on the first day when the US captain Hal Sutton made the baffling decision to pair Tiger Woods and Phil Mickelson – hardly the best of friends – in the Friday fourballs and foursomes. The pair lost both their matches on the opening day as Europe surged into a 6½-1½ lead. By the end of the second day, the lead had been stretched to 11-5.

The Americans needed the spirit of Brookline in the final day's singles, but Europe's players kept their nerve and condemned their opponents to their biggest loss on home soil.

Sergio Garcia disposed of Mickelson 3&2, while Lee Westwood defeated Kenny Perry 1 up. The stage was set for Colin Montgomerie, in only the sixth match out, to deliver the hammer blow against David Toms.

The 2006 and 2008 competitions saw comfortable wins for the home teams. First, a Darren Clarke-inspired Europe equalled their record-breaking winning margin on a highly emotional weekend at the K Club in Ireland. Captained by former Masters champion Ian Woosnam, the European team were imperious, none more so than Clarke, who had lost his wife Heather to cancer only the month before.

To have competed was one thing, to have dominated and won three points was another matter entirely. From the moment Clarke and his vanquished opponent Zach Johnson shook hands on the 16th hole to signal the Northern Irishman's victory, an emotional tidal wave rolled over the green. First to embrace Clarke was his caddie Billy Foster, followed by Tom Lehman, Ian Woosnam and then several players and caddies from both teams, as well as family and friends.

This incredibly emotional spectacle restored everyone's faith in the sport, and there was a feeling that the Ryder Cup had come full circle since 1999.

The 2008 competition held at Kentucky's Valhalla course saw Europe embarking on a quest to secure a fourth consecutive victory. However, it ended in a comfortable win for the Americans.

There was a minor undercurrent of animosity running through the weekend because the teams were captained by old rivals Paul Azinger and Nick Faldo. In Faldo (Europe's record points scorer and holder of the most appearances by any European), the away team were captained by someone whose insular nature made him one of the continent's greatest players but not one of its finest captains.

Europe had the better team and so for Faldo to guide them to defeat from such a position of strength was the mark of someone not cut out for leadership. Tony Jacklin he most certainly wasn't. In Paul Azinger, however, the Americans had the more astute and inspirational general, someone whose patriotic and outspoken nature helped lead his troops back to the promised land.

Faldo backloaded his team in the singles, sending out too many of his best players later on. With a better balance in his line-up, logic says Faldo would have cancelled out the 9-7 lead the US team took into the final day from the foursomes and fourballs, and then carved out a fourth consecutive European triumph. But it wasn't to be.

It was the younger players in the American side who caught the eye, especially the charismatic Boo Weekly and Anthony Kim. Their infectious nature and the 13th-man aspect of the local crowd carried the Americans over the line in a tournament to forget for the Europeans.

When play returned to Europe two years later the venue was Wales's Celtic Manor and the home side was captained by Mr Ryder Cup himself, Colin Montgomerie. One of the greatest exponents of the matchplay art, this was the event he was born to lead. It was the first time the event had been held in Wales and there was a sense that the home side had learned their lessons from Faldo's 2008 ordeal.

Horrendous weather over the weekend saw play suspended twice, meaning the competition went into Monday for the first time in its history, but not before the weekend had thrown up some glorious play. Europe found themselves 4-6 down after the first two sessions, but they fought back in blistering fashion to go into the final day's singles with a three-point lead.

As Montgomerie stated after the competition, the trophy was not won on Monday, but on Sunday when Europe collected 5½ points out of six and every member of the 12-man team contributed. In the end, Europe only scraped over the line with 14½ points; half a point less and the Ryder Cup would have returned to America.

It was US Open champion Graeme McDowell who sealed victory against Hunter Mahan in a tense finish on the penultimate hole, unleashing a seething mass of human celebration on the 17th green.

Victory had been bestowed on a captain once relentlessly ridiculed by the American galleries for his appearance and empty Major trophy cabinet. For Montgomerie and Europe it had unfolded in such a unique and special way that it will live long in the minds of those who were there.

Could this Welsh cliff-hanger ever be bettered? Few would have thought that possible, but how wrong they were. Everyone who followed the 2012 Ryder Cup at Chicago's Medinah Country Club could not fail to be united in the belief that this was one of the most unlikely and unexpected turnarounds that sport has yet produced.

Europe was captained by Seve's great friend and two-time Masters champion José Maria Olzábal, and the mood from the defending champions was upbeat. But, Ian Poulter aside, the team struggled over the first two days as the Americans, with Phil Mickelson and Keegan Bradley in outstanding form, raced into a commanding lead.

Going into the final day's singles, the European team trailed by 10 points to six and there was a palpable sense that the Americans would dispatch them without fuss on what had traditionally been their strongest day. But sometimes the presumption of victory can help to calm the nerves of the opposition and engineer an opportunity that can be grabbed with both hands. And this is precisely what the European team conspired to do with a dramatic 14½-13½ victory fuelled by an inspirational never-say-die spirit.

Every Ryder Cup throws up a hero or two, and this event was no different. For the third Ryder Cup in succession, Europe's talisman was Ian Poulter. Overwhelmingly self confident yet the epitome of patriotic pride, Poulter was unquestionably Ballesteros's representative on the course. "This Ryder Cup is not for the faint of heart," he proclaimed, and how right he was.

But Poulter's majestic four-point haul wasn't the only feat worthy of the highest praise. Step forward former Open champion Paul Lawrie, who thrashed an in-form Brad Snedeker 5&3, helped by arguably the shot of the week: a 40-foot chip in at the fourth hole.

And then there was Nicolas Colsaerts, who made a name for himself on the Friday when European heads were dropping courtesy of his laser-sighted putter, and Justin Rose. The point that Rose won against Phil Mickelson was unquestionably one of Europe's most pivotal.

Many times over the course of the 18 holes it looked like Rose was a beaten man but instead he sunk a succession of superb putts that gave the impression that Clark Kent had just walked onto the course.

On the final day, the Americans only needed 4½ points from the singles matches to regain the trophy but a front-loaded European side started strongly and had soon levelled the match. The final pairings saw the projected scores seesaw with nerve-shredding regularity as the combatants traded holes coming down the stretch. One moment America seemed assured of victory and the galleries reached fever pitch, the next, the Europeans had swung the balance in their favour and silenced the crowds. It was truly hide-behind-the-sofa-and-chew-your-nails stuff for the millions watching on TV.

However, the critical point was won by the ice-cool German Martin Kaymer. Kaymer, unlike Poulter, was an unlikely hero, coming off the back off a terrible six-month slump to beat Steve Stricker by draining a tough six-footer on the 18th. After countryman Bernhard Langer's agony at missing the crucial putt for the same prize 21 years earlier, the symmetry of this winning putt was impossible to escape.

The trophy was Europe's once more, the seventh victory in the last nine competitions. Seve would have been very proud.

Verdict: I would split this into two sections – pre Europe joining the fold and post. Therefore, pre: easily the Americans; post: the Europeans by way of a better record and a buccaneering, more courageous approach (not to mention two massive victories – in 2004 and 2006). Roll on 2014.

Daley Thompson

vs

Jürgen Hingsen

Throughout the 1980s, another sporting rivalry captured the imagination in much the same way as Ovett and Coe. This time, one of the combatants was British and the other German. One was brash and cocky, the other quiet and meticulous. Daley Thompson and Jürgen Hingsen were two of the finest athletes to grace the world of track and field, and they traded decathlon world records for much of the decade. Their seminal battles for supremacy at the Olympic Games and the World and European Championships are the stuff of athletics legend, where each meeting elevated the rivalry to unparalleled heights.

Francis Morgan Ayodélé Thompson was born in Notting Hill, West London, in 1958 to a Nigerian father and Scottish mother. (Daley is a contraction of Ayodélé, a Niger-Congo Yorùbá language word meaning 'joy comes home'.) He was sent to Farney Close boarding school in Sussex at the age of seven but promptly described the place as being only suitable for troubled children.

Thompson wanted to be a professional footballer but, like Steve Ovett, he found other members of the team wanting, so he joined Haywards Heath Harriers and switched his allegiance to athletics. He was a promising youngster blessed with great flat speed, so he was soon tipped for the shorter track events and the long jump. However, tragedy struck the family when he was only 12. His father, a taxi driver, was shot dead in Streatham,

South London.

Thompson returned to the capital in 1975 and joined the Essex Beagles. Coach Bob Mortimer recognised his potential and suggested he try the decathlon instead of concentrating on the sprints. Although initially sceptical about taking up the discipline, Thompson soon realised he had found his calling and never looked back. He competed in his first meeting in Wales later the same year and won easily. The following season he took the Amateur Athletics Association title and thus qualified for the 1976 Montreal Olympics (his score of 7684 points was the best ever recorded for a 17-year-old).

The Games clearly came a little too soon for the prodigiously talented youngster and he only finished 18th. Gold medallist and world record-holder Bruce Jenner had recognised his potential, however, and he took Thompson back to California after the Games to pass the baton to the young upstart. Thompson's star was clearly on the rise and the following year he took the European Junior title. In 1978 he won the first of three Commonwealth gold medals in Edmonton, Canada. It is a mark of just how far he had come in a short space of time that he notched up 8467 points. Australia's Peter Hadfield took silver with 7623, so Thompson was clearly a very special athlete indeed.

He had minor hiccups later in 1978 when, despite a strong first day he faded to finish fourth at the European Championships in Prague (a performance which scarred him for years) and in 1979 when he failed to finish his only decathlon of the year. But Thompson was such a formidable long jumper that he won the UK Championships in that discipline instead, cementing his status as a multi-talented athlete. Thompson was now entering his peak years and from 1980 onwards his rivalry with Hingsen became the stuff of sporting legend.

Jürgen Hingsen was born in Duisburg, Germany, in 1958. He began his career as a jumper of some distinction but, having discussed the decathlon with Thompson at a junior international match in Bremen in 1976 when they were both competing in the long jump, Hingsen decided to switch to the multi-discipline event. Thompson wouldn't have to wait long to lock horns with his new adversary – the following year they met at the European

Junior Championships. The friendly banter was a thing of the past because of their newly acquired status as direct rivals.

Although established decathlete Guido Kratschmer had reached his peak and was on the slide, Hingsen and Siegfried 'Siggi' Wentz still gave the Germans a strong presence. Hingsen, known at home as the 'German Hercules', made an immediate impact on the discipline by winning an Under 19 competition against a strong Russian team in 1977. Whereas Thompson had no direct domestic rivals, Hingsen benefited enormously from the stiff competition from Kratschmer and Wentz and his results formed a steep upward curve. He broke the 8000-point barrier for the first time in Krefeld in 1979, but he was denied his first significant chance to defeat Thompson when the West German team boycotted the 1980 Olympics.

By the beginning of the 1980 season, Thompson was in prime condition to challenge for the Olympic title. He set a new world record of 8622 points in Götzis in Austria before heading to Moscow. Although he tried to ignore events in the wider world, it annoyed him that the Americans and West Germans boycotted the Games because of Soviet intervention in Afghanistan. It meant that his greatest rivals, particularly Hingsen and Kratschmer, wouldn't be there to challenge him.

Thompson put the disappointment out of his mind and told himself that people only remembered who won the gold medal, not who was missing from the competition. He started well and clocked 10.62 in the 100 metres in the Lenin Stadium. He backed this up with an 8-metre long jump, and by the end of the first day was well ahead of the East Germans and Russians. The second day was even easier and Thompson treated the 1500 metres as a few laps of honour. He could have tried for the world record (which Kratschmer had taken before the Olympics) but elected not to bother. A crowd that had not been particularly responsive to Westerners during the Games gave him a standing ovation, so the charismatic Thompson responded by conducting them during the national anthem.

The following year was relatively quiet by Thompson's standards but 1982 was a different matter. This was when Hingsen came to the fore and became a serious threat to his dominance. As a physical specimen, Hingsen was hard to match.

He stood six feet seven inches (two metres) tall and was powerfully built. He excelled in the jumps and the throws because of his build, although he was less comfortable in the sprints.

"He strikes me as being a bit arrogant but I probably strike him as being incredibly arrogant. I respect him as a decathlete because he's good, but it's impossible to be close friends when you're after the same thing." Daley Thompson

Both men returned to Götzis in the build-up to the 1982 European Championships, but it was Thompson who came out on top with a world record-breaking performance. In the press conference afterwards he fielded several general questions as well as a few about Sebastian Coe and Steve Ovett, who seemed to be hogging the limelight with their world records in the middle distances. Thompson was his usual cocky self: "I'm better at my event than they are at theirs because they have rivals who can get close to them whereas no one can get close to me."

Hingsen had finished second to Thompson, but he snatched the world record a few weeks later in the West German National Championships in Ulm with a mammoth total of 8723. He didn't like to goad the Brit so remained quiet about an achievement that had clearly shocked Thompson. Steve Ovett countered on his behalf, however: "The decathlon is nine Mickey Mouse events and a slow 1500 metres."

The upcoming Thompson-Hingsen clash at the European Championships in Athens was now attracting considerable interest. Hingsen had the world record and Thompson had never been under this kind of pressure before. The order of events in the decathlon always gave Thompson as the runner-long jumper a head-start, however. There's no doubt that during the course of their careers this affected Hingsen psychologically, because he was always a hundred or more points behind after the 100 metres and the long jump, Thompson's two strongest events. The muscular Hingsen was a powerful shot-putter and closed the gap slightly, and he closed it further with a superb 2.15-metre leap in the high jump. Thompson then extended his lead after a solid 400 metres.

Day two saw an inspired Thompson force home his advantage over a mentally shot Hingsen. The German crumbled under the pressure and his discus, javelin and pole vault were all well below par. Now all Thompson needed to cement his status as the best all-round athlete was to run sub-4.28 for the 1500 metres and he'd reclaim the world record from the German. As so often happened in major championships Thompson delivered, running 4.23.7 to set a new total of 8744 points. At the end of the race the other athletes collapsed onto the track, while Thompson stood amongst them like a sporting colossus.

The following month Thompson flew to Brisbane for the defence of his Commonwealth Games title. He landed to a media storm about his refusal to carry the English flag at the opening ceremony, but Thompson knew the six-hour extravaganza would interfere with his preparation so he stuck to his guns. Although he didn't perform particularly well, he still took the gold.

In 1983 Thompson suffered a compression injury to his back and then a torn abductor muscle and he wasn't expected to challenge the Germans at the inaugural World Championships in Helsinki. He persuaded national coach Frank Dick to take him to the games on the condition that no one could let Hingsen know he was injured. Thompson was left with no option but to train in private while Hingsen posed for photos, signed autographs for the fans and even consented to interviews with the British media.

The night before the competition, Thompson sat down with his friend, the American sprinter Marti Krules, and worked out how fast, how far and how high he would need to go in every event to beat Hingsen. The next morning Thompson was bouncing around the warm-up area in good spirits while Hingsen was cold and aloof. Thompson wasn't trying to psyche out his opponent, but he knew that Hingsen would wonder what all the fuss was about and might take his mind off the important business of winning.

The casual approach worked because Hingsen seemed preoccupied and, if anything, too tense. As usual, Thompson was ahead after the opening two events and he also had a good high jump. Hingsen fought back in the shot, 400 metres and hurdles but Thompson, showing relatively few signs of discomfort from the injury, extended his lead in the discus and pole vault. After a disappointing javelin, Hingsen was left with too much to do in the 1500 metres and he again took silver to Thompson's gold, with Wentz finishing third.

This victory meant that Thompson became the first man to hold the British, European, Commonwealth, World and Olympic titles simultaneously, a quite startling achievement. Hingsen could only respond in one way, and that was by reclaiming the world record, which he managed in Bernhausen (8779 points) shortly afterwards, and then again at Mannheim in early 1984 (8798).

The fact that Hingsen had bested his points tally only inspired Thompson to greater heights and he approached the 1984 Los Angeles Olympics in good form. This would be the defining confrontation of their careers. Thompson, Hingsen and Kratschmer were drawn in the same heat for the 100 metres, but it was Thompson who landed the first psychological blow with a personal best of 10.44 seconds. Hingsen then posted a 7.80-metre long jump, which Thompson could only match with his first two jumps. With his final attempt, however, he soared out to 8.01m, another personal best. Thompson had the bit between his teeth and he wasn't going to hand Hingsen the advantage in the German's best events. He recorded yet another PB in the shot, although Hingsen clawed back some of the deficit with a solid high jump. Thompson ended the first day with a blistering 400 metres and took a 114-point advantage into the second day.

Hingsen was usually much stronger over the hurdles and he duly won the event in 14.29 seconds. If their decade-long rivalry could be encapsulated in a single event, however, it would be the discus in Los Angeles. Hingsen threw first and recorded a personal best of 49.80 metres, while Thompson threw poorly and could only manage 37.90 metres. Hingsen then extended his advantage by going over 50 metres. Thompson, on the other hand, hardly improved. Hingsen's third throw was no better but he would still glean 886 points for his second throw while Thompson would only net 710 if he failed to improve. This would give Hingsen the lead for the first time in their seven meetings and he would hold the psychological edge going into the home straight.

Crunch time.

Thompson knew his place in Olympic history rode on one throw of the discus. He entered the cage muttering to himself and swinging his arms to relieve some of the tension. Then he set himself, rotated briskly across the circle and whipped his arm round with ferocious power. The discus sailed out to 46.56 metres, yet another personal best in competition. Thompson had faced the toughest moment in his career with characteristic determination and relieved all the pressure with a moment of pure magic. Instead of being behind, he still held a slender lead going into the pole vault.

Now Hingsen was under pressure and, once again, he crumbled. (Despite having the edge in six of the ten events – from a personal best point of view – Hingsen never managed to deliver consistently, otherwise he would surely have beaten Thompson. Indeed, added together, the points from his PBs yielded a total of 9323 to Thompson's 9315.) In the pole vault, Hingsen could only manage 4.50 metres, while Thompson cleared 5 metres. As he was performing his now-iconic back-flip on the landing mat in front of a packed Los Angeles Coliseum, Hingsen was finding the tension unbearable and was throwing up in the tunnel leading out of the stadium.

"It's not enough for Daley to win, he has to destroy his opponent mentally." Sebastian Coe

Thompson knew the damage had been done and he promptly beat Hingsen in the javelin to ensure the 1500 metres would be yet another victory parade. The only question that remained was whether he would break Hingsen's world record as easily as he had broken the man himself. Thompson did not view reclaiming the record as his priority, however. He had said from the outset that his goal was to win three Olympic decathlon titles and he only did enough to secure the second. Some believe that by leaving the record in Hingsen's hands, Thompson gave himself something to aim at in future competitions, and because he knew he could break it, this would play havoc with Hingsen's mind. (As it happened, the scoring tables were recalculated shortly after the Olympics and Thompson was credited with a world record of 8847 points, which stood until broken by American

Dan O'Brien in 1992.)

"He (Hingsen) *scored the most ever points by a loser, so I don't think he did too badly."* Daley Thompson

"Daley had that extreme will to win – he never let you relax." Jürgen Hingsen

Controversy and Thompson went hand in hand throughout his career and the aftermath of the Los Angeles Olympics was no exception. He first wore a T-shirt castigating the host broadcasters' obsession with the American athletes, then whistled during the national anthem and finally wore a T-shirt to a press conference asking 'Is the world's second greatest athlete gay?', a crass reference to the rumours circulating about Carl Lewis. Thompson's humour was often cruel and he was also accused of having no kindness or grace by opponents and commentators alike. But that was all part of what made Thompson the ultra-competitive animal.

"Hingsen seems to be pretty good at ringing up the points at a nice easy meeting at home in Germany, but Thompson prefers the head-to-head competition. What he's got isn't physical, it's mental. Whatever happens, he responds by performing better. He's much more of a fighter." NBC broadcaster Frank Zarnowski

Thompson wanted to use the 1986 Commonwealth Games, European Championships and the 1987 World Championships as a springboard to the 1988 Seoul Olympics and sporting immortality but things didn't turn out quite as he had planned. He duly secured gold in Edinburgh and then beat Hingsen to the gold in Stuttgart but he was injured for the World Championships the following year and they were a disappointment: he could only finish ninth, his first defeat in all competitions in nine years. Hingsen failed to finish and it looked like both men had had their day.

The pair dragged themselves to the Olympics but both were to be disappointed again, none more so than Hingsen after he false started in the 100 metres and was disqualified from the whole event. Thompson, too, was having problems. His sprint was strong but he was a good half-metre down in the long jump and ten centimetres from respectability in the high jump. With his hopes of an unprecedented third consecutive gold fading, he ran a slow 400 metres and hurdles and then his pole snapped in the vault, injuring his fingers and left thigh. He couldn't overcome the injury in the 1500 metres, even though equalling his personal best would have given him the gold. The final positions saw Thompson and Hingsen finish fourth and fifth respectively in the last major event at which they would go head to head, a frustrating end to two illustrious careers.

The two men traded world records for most of the decade and came to define their sport. Hingsen's eight victories from 28 starts doesn't compare favourably with Thompson's 19 from 31, but without each other the sport would have been much the poorer and they inspired one another to greater heights. Indeed, nearly 25 years on, Thompson's 8847 points and Hingsen's 8832 see them still comfortably in the top ten on the all-time list (and either score would have won gold at the 2008 Olympics in Beijing).

Verdict: Although Hingsen took the world record on three occasions, the pair met ten times in competition and Thompson came out on top every time. He remains arguably the greatest multi-discipline exponent of all time.

Muhammad Ali

vs

Joe Frazier

"I always bring out the best in men I fight, but Joe Frazier, I'll tell the world right now, brings out the best in me. I'm gonna tell ya, that's one helluva man, and God bless him." Ali, after the 'Thrilla in Manila'

When contemplating which rivalries to focus on in this book, several came close to making the cut; others made it by the skin of their sporting teeth. But from the first conversation to the final decision, one rose above the parapet more than any other: Muhammad Ali versus Smokin' Joe Frazier.

To anyone with more than a passing interest in the history of the sport it is as if they were permanently linked, always connected by a hyphen, impossible to say one name without muttering the other. One a garrulous Adonis of coruscating technique and guile with all the elegance of a Tennyson poem, the other a warrior hewn from Philadelphian granite with immeasurable strength and a left hook that could fell Goliath.

Theirs was a rivalry that surpassed Sugar Ray Robinson and Jake La Motta, Tommy Hearns and Sugar Ray Leonard, and Tony Zale and Rocky Graziano combined. Their trilogy of antagonism-filled duels consisted of some of the most breathtaking and brutal fighting ever witnessed, and the verbal sparring that each bout threw up echoed the social issues of the day and polarised the American people.

The rivalry began when Ali – born Cassius Clay before he joined the Nation of Islam and changed his name – was languishing in boxing limbo. He had been exiled by the Boxing Commission after his refusal to report for selective service for the ongoing war in Vietnam, claiming that his religious beliefs forbade him from taking another person's life.

After memorably winning the 1960 light heavyweight Olympic gold medal in Rome, Ali then shocked the boxing fraternity with his sixth-round win over the seemingly unbeatable champion Sonny 'Big Ugly Bear' Liston on February 25th, 1964, which he followed up with a first-round victory in the rematch in May 1965. Ali's great hand speed in the second fight saw him fell Liston with a punch that was so fast that half the fans in the audience never saw it. Neither did Liston.

However, the braggadocio and outspoken beliefs of the unbeaten Ali brought with them many detractors. And it was this refusal to join up for military service (*"No Vietcong ever called me nigger"*) that gave his detractors the ammunition they needed to use against him.

So, stripped of his title, the WBA and WBC set out to find a new champion. After an eight-man boxing tournament organised by the WBA was won by Jimmy Ellis, and a WBC deciding bout between Buster Mathis and Joe Frazier was won by Frazier, a fight was arranged between Frazier and Ellis to decide supremacy in the vacant division, which Frazier duly won.

However, many perceived the Philadelphia-born Frazier as a mere pretender to Ali's crown, and Ali's unbeaten record and enforced exile only served to compound the theory. It was to Frazier's eternal credit that he appeared to agree with the naysayers and, wanting to escape the heavy shadow that Ali cast over him, he publicly supported Ali in his quest to be reinstated by the Boxing Commission. He even lent Ali money to continue his legal battle. During this early period both men remained friendly, Frazier publicly praising Ali as a great champion. It wasn't to last.

In 1970, after three years entrenched in the boxing wilderness, Ali won his court case and was acquitted of all charges. He immediately went into training to fight Frazier. Before he was ready to step toe to toe with the world's 'official' unbeaten heavyweight champion, Ali fought two tough fights to make sure he was in the right shape. First up was Jerry Quarry: 'The Great White Hope' – appropriate given Ali's imminent but nonetheless surprising verbal attacks on Frazier – was dispatched convincingly.

Shortly after his tussle with Quarry, the New York State Supreme Court ruled that Ali had been unjustly denied a boxing licence. So, able to fight again in New York, he fought Oscar Bonavena at Madison Square Garden in December 1970. After 14 gruelling rounds, Ali stopped Bonavena in the 15th, paving the way for the 'big one'.

It was after this victory and in the lead-up to this long-awaited fight that Ali changed dramatically. He embarked on a series of verbal onslaughts so truculent that they took the reigning champion completely by surprise. He was known as someone who would psychologically unhinge his opponents in the days prior to the fights with all manner of barbs, some whimsical, some downright personal, but this was different. As well as mocking his opponent's skill and looks, he called Frazier an Uncle Tom – a disparaging slang term for a black man who acts in a passive, subservient manner toward white people.

Ali believed he was justified in his damning approach as Frazier's contract had been purchased by a conglomerate of white-owned corporations. Plus, Frazier had been extremely reluctant to voice any opinions on civil rights' issues. Suffice to say this did not sit well with the outspoken Ali.

Unsurprisingly, Frazier took these slurs personally, especially after all the help he had given Ali (a man he would respectfully refer to as 'Butterfly' at times) during his exile. The effect that these attacks had on boxing fans (and indeed some non-boxing fans) manifested itself in a black-white supporting group.

Black people and young people lined up behind Ali; older more conservative whites behind Frazier. This polarisation was typical of the society of the day and conjured up an unpleasant backdrop to the first fight that, to this day, leaves a nasty taste in the mouth.

When the fight finally happened at New York's iconic Madison Square Garden on March 8th, 1971 it was the most eagerly anticipated fight of all time and the hottest ticket in town. It was an event that transcended boxing: two undefeated champions fighting for supremacy, both with a newly found hatred for each other.

So electrifying was the sense of anticipation that ringside was crammed with the most famous celebrities of the day. Frank Sinatra, who couldn't get a ticket, had persuaded *Life* magazine to hire him as their official photographer, while Burt Lancaster, who had never commentated on a fight in his life, was given a microphone to act as co-commentator for the closed-circuit TV broadcast.

Ali started strongly, dominating Frazier with his incredible speed of hand, foot and eye. Frazier, never a fighter to back off, rallied immediately. He landed barrage after barrage of thunderous body shots to Ali's midriff. Level going into the 11th round, Frazier caught Ali with a monstrous left hook that robbed Ali of his senses and had him slumping into the ropes. He somehow survived the round but the damage was done. Frazier took control of the fight and another spectacular left hook in the final round sent Ali crashing to the canvas for only the third time in his glittering career.

This foudroyant blow was like a bolt of lightning to Ali. Yet to the surprise of those who knew that a ferocious knockdown from Frazier meant you were not getting back up, Ali did just that. And despite a flurry of earth-moving blows from his opponent in the latter stages of the round, Ali stayed on his feet until the bell.

Frazier won a unanimous decision and ended Ali's vaunted unbeaten record.

A battle of epic proportions, no heavyweight title fight has ever matched its dramatic sustained action, and to this day it is still referred to as the 'Fight of the Century'.

Ali, somewhat predictably, disputed the decision, claiming the referee and judges (who were all white) were biased. He also used every verbal tactic in his book to throw a veil of doubt over the outcome and, more to the point, engineer a rematch. However, circumstances elsewhere conspired to take the matter out of his hands.

On January 22nd, 1973, the delightfully titled 'Sunshine

Showdown' between Frazier and the dominating George Foreman took place in the Jamaican capital, Kingston. Despite Foreman's formidable size and reach, undefeated champion Frazier was odds on to win the fight. However, just two minutes into the first round things changed emphatically when Foreman knocked Frazier to the canvas.

"Down goes Frazier! Down goes Frazier!" shouted HBO's lauded commentator Howard Cosell. With just under thirty seconds left in the round, Foreman floored the champion again. He went on to brutalise Frazier, knocking him down four more times. After the sixth knockdown, referee Arthur Mercante decided enough was enough and stopped Frazier from continuing, awarding victory to Foreman by technical knockout and handing him the title after one of the sport's greatest upsets.

No one could have imagined they'd see Frazier manhandled like that, least of all Frazier himself. He desperately wanted a rematch against Foreman, but Ali pointed out that Frazier had already had his shot and failed, so it was now his turn to tackle the new champion.

There was only one way to settle the dispute, the result of which gave Ali the best of both worlds: he was given the chance to challenge Foreman for his title, plus the opportunity to avenge his defeat at Frazier's hands. The rematch with Frazier was hastily arranged.

Fewer than three years had passed since their first titanic encounter, and in that time Ali had fought 13 times, most memorably against Ken Norton twice, losing the first fight – in which Norton broke Ali's jaw – before winning the rematch. Frazier, however, had only fought four times in the same period, twice before his Foreman loss, and a 12-round win against Joe Bugner in London afterwards.

However, if Frazier thought that Ali had calmed down after the first fight then the build up to the second fight quickly dispelled that notion. Ali resumed his usual shenanigans with a declaration of verbal warfare. When the two met face-to-face during a televised interview for ABC, Ali so infuriated Frazier that Frazier had to be restrained. While he was being calmed, Ali abruptly tackled him to the floor and the two started wrestling on air. Studio security finally intervened to separate them.

It was clear in the weeks leading up to the second fight, however, that it lacked the drama and media frenzy of the first match, primarily because there was no title on the line, and neither man was undefeated any more. However, the palpable animosity between the two ensured that the event was still a major draw.

And so on January 28th, 1974, the feud entered its second phase, again at Madison Square Garden. Ali, much like the initial contest, started the fight well; he was light on his feet and made sure that he constantly circled Frazier's fearsome left hook. When he got close, Ali would cut loose with quick fire combinations, and he took the first two rounds with ease.

Frazier seemed a little off his game after his humiliating loss to Foreman, while Ali was fighting an uncharacteristically cautious fight. He was later criticised for holding Frazier too often (an unsportsmanlike tactic designed to prevent an opponent from delivering effective body blows) which further threw Frazier. The comparatively lacklustre fight – comfortably the least entertaining of their trilogy – ended with Ali winning unanimously on points.

Ali was a happy man. Not only had he defeated his bitter rival, he was now the number one contender for Foreman's world title. The much-hyped Ali-Foreman match took place in Kinshasa in Zaire on October 30th, 1974. Although Ali, now 32, had bested the only two people to defeat him – Norton and Frazier – he was still the overwhelming underdog against Foreman's awesome power. Ali once again proved that he had some surprises left however.

In what would become known as 'The Rumble in the Jungle', Ali started in his usual sprightly manner, landing a few aggressive blows. Foreman soon countered, landing several powerful hits of his own. His devastating power was rocking an Ali who clearly couldn't walk through the blows to outbox his opponent; he needed a different tactic, and what was to follow was one of the most inventive and clinical changes in style ever seen.

As the second round unfolded, Ali began to cover up and lean on the ropes, fielding Foreman's punches on the arms and body. This strategy would later be termed rope-a-dope. While trying to break through Ali's impregnable guard, Foreman was expending energy at a furious rate.

Every time Foreman drew back for a breather, Ali shot quick, accurate punches into face. While in clinches, he would taunt his opponent (*"Is that all you've got, George? Is that it?"*), enraging him further. Then with seconds left in the eighth round, Ali struck. A five-punch combination culminated with a left hook and a hard right. Foreman was down and out.

Ali was the world heavyweight champion for the second time, and the stage was set for the third and final fight between the new champion and his long-time nemesis. It was a fight that would go down in boxing annals as arguably the greatest heavyweight bout ever staged.

The promotional creation of Don King and Bob Arum, the fight's incongruous location was the Philippine capital. There was only one reason for choosing Manila: money. Ferdie Pacheco, Ali's cornerman and physician, recalled the general opinion about the seminal fight: "The first fight was life and death, and Frazier won. Second fight: Ali figures him out no problem. Then Ali beats Foreman and Frazier's sun sets...all of us thought Frazier was shot. We all thought Manila would be an easy fight."

How wrong they were.

The usual pre-fight name-calling didn't disappoint. Ali, if anything, went further than he had previously, unleashing ruthless diatribes at Frazier and calling him a gorilla. Frazier, fuelled by both pride and hatred retorted: "I want to hurt him. If I knock him down, I'll stand back, give him a chance to breathe. It's his heart I want."

When the night of the fight came, the heat was oppressive. But the conditions did nothing to diminish the pace of the action and the ubiquity of the brutal blows that rained down on both gladiators. The sustained violence has never been bettered in a fight since, a rampant show of pugilism that would never have existed if it wasn't for the antagonism between the two fighters and the almost superman stamina and courage that they shared.

Despite the inevitable quick start for Ali, Frazier kept coming. At one point he caught Ali with a left hook so ferocious it was hard to comprehend how Ali's head didn't fly off. Ali looked at Frazier and said: "They told me Joe Frazier was all washed up."

Frazier shot back: "They lied."

As this tidal wave of intensity entered the 12th round it changed course. Ali repeatedly shook Frazier with mammoth blows that, according to Michael Parkinson at ringside, sounded like car doors being slammed and culminated in an astonishing left hook that knocked Frazier's mouth guard into the crowd. By the end of the 14th round, Frazier's left eye was so swollen that he could no longer see (it emerged afterwards that he had been partially blind in his right eye for many years, so for the later rounds he hadn't been able to see at all).

Before the bell went for the final round, Eddie Futch, Frazier's trainer, stopped the fight with the immortal words: "It's all over. No one will ever forget what you did here today." He knew Frazier couldn't go on even if there were only three minutes left. It was an act of compassion that has been praised ever since: a trainer ensuring his man would take no more punishment. Little did Futch know that Ali was also running on empty and had just asked Angelo Dundee to cut off his gloves. For him the stoppage came at just at the right time, and he promptly collapsed in his corner. A titanic trilogy over, Ali was still the champion. But only just.

"They weren't fighting for the heavyweight championship of the world – they were fighting for the heavyweight championship of each other." Jerry Izenberg

Neither man was the same fighter again. Frazier wouldn't win another fight after Manila, which included another defeat at the hands of George Foreman. Ali dodged a rematch against Foreman and instead peppered his remaining years in the game with what he thought would be easier fights, but battles such as those against Chuck Wepner (the inspiration for the *Rocky* films) and Earnie Shavers were anything but.

Ali went on to lose three of his last four fights, and his brutal defeats against Larry Holmes and Trevor Berbick came at a point when he should have been enjoying retirement. Indeed his voice was already slurred and his mannerisms hinted at the

Parkinson's diagnosis that was to follow. It was a sad end to the greatest of all fighting careers.

In more than forty years since their first incredible fight at the Garden, Frazier had nothing good to say about Ali. He seemed to revel in the fact that Ali ended up with Parkinson's disease, considering it Karmic justice for all the terrible things that Ali said about him. However, Frazier could never boast Ali's vast fortune and went bankrupt in his later years. Before his death in late 2011, he was living in a small room over his gym.

For his part, Ali seemed to realise the error of his ways later in life, as well as what he had inadvertently achieved: "I said a lot of things in the heat of the moment that I shouldn't have said. I called him names I shouldn't have called him. I apologise for that. I'm sorry. It was all meant to promote the fight."

When in more reflective mood, Frazier had gone on record saying: "The Butterfly and me have been through some ups and downs and there have been lots of emotions, many of them bad. But I have forgiven him. I had to. You cannot hold out forever. There were bruises in my heart because of the words he used. I spent years dreaming about him and wanting to hurt him. But you have got to throw that stick out of the window. Do not forget that we needed each other to produce some of the greatest fights of all time."

Verdict: Ali and Frazier's legacy is one that transcends all sport. Ali is universally regarded as the most beautiful fighter boxing has seen, perhaps the greatest athlete of all time. Meanwhile, Frazier's strength, resolve and bravery elevate him, with only a select few for company, into the pantheon of extraordinary fighters. Their rivalry is the stuff of legend and, together, their three monumental bouts and 41 rounds of spellbinding entertainment and seemingly non-stop visceral, breathtaking action will forever be etched in the minds of those who saw them. A rivalry without peer: two fighters, one historical entry.

Holland

vs

Germany

No sport can come close to the number of rivalries boasted by football and it is almost impossible to separate the plethora of domestic head-to-heads. However, there is one rich yet bitter international rivalry that stands head and shoulders above all others.

The English believe their football rivalry with Germany is felt as keenly on the continent, but the Germans actually have a more deeply embedded and fiercer rivalry with the Dutch. As with many team sport rivalries, the seeds were sown during wartime. Despite the Dutch declaring themselves neutral, the German army occupied the Netherlands for five years in the Second World War, during which a quarter of a million Dutch were killed, and deep-seated feelings of resentment have existed between the two ever since.

There were several non-competitive matches between the nations between the end of hostilities and the 1974 World Cup in Germany, but the Germans were by far the superior team. (They thrashed the Netherlands 7-0 in Cologne in 1959 and beat them again, 4-2, in Rotterdam in 1966.) The Dutch didn't enter or couldn't qualify for any World Cup between 1950 and 1970, and they didn't appear at the European Championships until 1976.

Germany, on the other hand, caused an almighty stir in the 1954 World Cup when they beat Ferenc Puskas's seemingly unstoppable Hungarian Magyars 3-2 in the final. Two-nil down after just eight minutes, they rallied quickly to level matters ten minutes later, before sneaking an unlikely victory with a late winner. Germany were world champions, the players immortalised after the Miracle of Bern. They came fourth in 1958, before losing 'that' final in 1966 and emerging the wrong side of a gripping seven-goal semi-final thriller against a Rivera-inspired Italy in 1970.

Holland finally made it to the top table of European football via club side Ajax and their mercurial playmaker – and all-time great – Johan Cruyff. And a period of Dutch dominance was ushered in when, in 1970, Feyenoord beat Celtic in the European Cup final. Ajax then went on to win the prestigious club championship for the next three years. The balance of power was clearly moving west.

They were still lagging behind the Germans on the international stage, however. At the 1972 European Championships in Belgium, a strong West Germany, led by Franz Beckenbauer (Der Kaiser – The Emperor) and spearheaded by the lethal Gerd Müller (Der Bomber – The Bomber), trounced the Soviet Union 3-0 in the final. Meanwhile, on the domestic front, a Bayern Munich side that contained many of the stars of the German national team overtook Ajax to emerge as the strongest club side in Europe.

The first time the two nations met in a competitive football match was in the 1974 FIFA World Cup final at Munich's Olympic Stadium, and the Dutch were intent on humiliating their opponents. Germany's occupation was within living memory for many fans, plus the Dutch were furious about an unscrupulous German newspaper piece printed a week before the game, which involved a false accusation against the Dutch team over a secret orgy.

The Dutch had swept all before them, including South American giants Argentina and Brazil, and had only conceded one goal before the final. Their mesmerising and adventurous 'total football', engineered by their legendary coach Rinus Michels, had captured the imagination. They attacked with 10 men, and if they lost the ball then defended with 11, and with the likes of Rudi Krol, Johnny Rep, Johan Neeskens and the magician himself, Cruyff, in their ranks they were hotly tipped to win their first world crown.

The Germans, on the other hand, had progressed steadily, but on home soil and with Beckenbauer, Overath, Hoeness and goal machine Müller in their prime, a Dutch victory was far from guaranteed.

The match started well for the Dutch and it was only a minute old when Cruyff ghosted past three defenders before being brought down in the box by Hoeness. Neeskens stepped up and scored from the spot to give them an early lead, which was all the more galling for their opponents as the Germans hadn't touched the ball. Midfielder Willem van Hanegem, a man who had lost his father and two brothers during a bombing raid, clenched his fists in delight: "I didn't give a damn about the score. One-nil was enough as long as we could humiliate them. I hate them. They murdered my family."

The Dutch proceeded to toy with their opponents, a grave error against a German side renowned for its unremitting resolve. It was as if they had forgotten one of the golden rules of sport: being the best is not an acceptable alternative to victory. And it was no surprise that their hubris was punished when the Germans equalised, also from the spot, after Bernd Hölzenbein burst into the box but then appeared to dive under a soft challenge from Wim Jansen. England's Jack Taylor awarded the penalty and Paul Breitner calmly stroked home the equaliser.

Gerd Müller then gave the Germans the lead just before half-time. Rainer Bonhof broke down the right and squared the ball to Müller, but he took the ball with his back to goal and didn't appear to be able to get a shot away. However, Müller, with his low centre of gravity and agility of a ballerina, spun on a sixpence and, with perfect balance and timing, fired a low shot past the helpless Jan Jongbloed.

The Dutch immediately threw everything at the Germans. There was still time in the first half for Rep to be presented with an open goal after a weaving run by Cruyff. However, the usually clinical Rep froze, his shot hitting the helpless 'keeper, Sepp Maier.

As the second-half got underway, the Dutch continued their siege but they simply couldn't find a way through the German defence, and when they did they found Maier in inspirational form. When the final whistle blew the stadium erupted but the Dutch were completely shell-shocked.

Having been strong favourites and confident of strolling to victory, the Dutch were distraught, the nation traumatised by 'De moeder aller nederlagen' or 'The mother of all defeats'. Twenty years after vanquishing a team regarded as the most entertaining in football history, the Germans had done it again, world champions for the second time.

All subsequent Bayern Munich-Ajax encounters in European club football took on a greater significance as a result. Bayern went on to match Ajax's three consecutive European Cups and the national team prospered as a consequence: West Germany reached the final of the 1976 European Championships and only lost to Czechoslovakia after a penalty shootout.

The two didn't meet again in a competitive international until the second group stage of the 1978 World Cup in Argentina. German striker Karl-Heinz Rummenigge knew the Dutch would be out to avenge their earlier defeat: "The pressure was tremendous. The popular press was blowing up the old rivalry. We knew that on the pitch the Dutch were ready and waiting for us. We had to stay focused. I think it's a shame that they regard football as an outlet for their hatred from the Second World War."

The Dutch, however, were this time shorn of their talisman, Cruyff. In mysterious circumstances, Cruyff announced that he would not be travelling to South America, and the truth behind his decision would only emerge thirty years later, when he announced that after a foiled kidnap attempt on his family he had changed his attitude to life and decided not to play in the World Cup.

The match ended 2-2, a late René van de Kerkhof strike saving the game for the Dutch. Although they hadn't beaten Germany for 22 years, this goal contributed to Germany's elimination from the tournament. The Dutch made the final and, had Rob Rensenbrink's strike not hit the post and bounced out with a minute on the clock, they surely would have beaten hosts Argentina to lift the World Cup. Instead, the game went to extra time and Mario Kempes secured a 3-1 win for the home side.

Many of the same players took the field for an ill-tempered

group-stage match in the 1980 European Championships in Naples, Italy. This time German midfielder Karl-Heinz Förster stirred the pot pre-match: "Before the game we knew that it was going to be tense. We had sworn to win because that victory was so important for our sense of pride. To them, beating us is the best thing there is. They hate us so much more than we hate them."

The match had barely begun when Johnny Rep hit German goalkeeper Harald 'Toni' Schumacher, a man who once beat Hitler into second place in an unpopularity contest after his dreadful challenge on France's Patrick Battiston during the 1982 World Cup. Schumacher then ended up fighting with Dutch defender Huub Stevens. And when van de Kerkhof realised his late goal wasn't going to salvage the game, he punched opposing midfielder Bernd Schuster. Germany eventually won the brawl 3-2, with Klaus Allofs netting a hat-trick for the Germans. They also went on to lift the trophy, beating Belgium in the final.

The 1980s were a low point for both domestic and international football. Hooliganism was on the rise and the game had to take a backseat after the Heysel disaster and a number of high-profile matches were blighted by fans at war. A year before Heysel, the two nations organised a ten-year anniversary friendly of the 1974 World Cup final to try to retrieve some of the lost spirit of the game.

With 21 of the 22 players from the previous match returning, it was sure to be a keenly fought contest. Cruyff promised to show the world that the Dutch should have won and he duly scored the only goal of the game, but the match didn't really capture the imagination and left fans in little doubt that it was a sideshow when compared with their full international rivalry.

The Dutch failed to qualify for three consecutive tournaments in the mid-1980s but they did make it to Germany for Euro '88. They were still out to avenge the Naples result and were handed their chance when they squared up against the hosts in the semi-final in Hamburg. The German FA generously allocated the Dutch fans 6000 tickets but thousands more managed to procure them on the black market and the stadium was awash with orange. In the first half the Dutch showed their class and, although they failed to score, they made the Germans look like schoolboys. Their failure to find the net, however, almost came back to haunt them.

In the second half the Germans had clearly adopted dirty tactics and set out to unsettle the Dutch with cynical tackling and more aggressive body language. They also apparently resorted to taunting the Dutch black players with racist slurs. The Dutch, somewhat predictably, fell into the trap and retaliated. Lothar Matthäus gave Germany the lead from the spot after serial sniper victim Jürgen Klinsmann again went down easily, but late goals from Ronald Koeman – another dubious penalty – and the clinical Marco van Basten secured the win for the visitors.

At the final whistle, as was tradition, the teams swapped shirts. Koeman then caused outrage in Germany by appearing to wipe his backside with Olaf Thon's jersey, something he later claimed to have done for real. He then tried to justify his behaviour by saying that none of the German players had shaken his hand or congratulated his team. (Only Beckenbauer boarded the Dutch bus to offer his congratulations, although he later said they hadn't deserved to win.) For once, the normally critical Dutch press didn't care. They even praised some of the dubious tackling and poor sportsmanship.

For the Dutch people there was a massive outpouring of relief; for the Germans only the bitter taste of defeat. The Dutch fans saw their team as the resistance, the Germans, with their eagles on their chests, as the Wehrmacht. Only this time they had invaded the Fatherland in their thousands and defeated the old enemy. In their eyes, good was finally prevailing over evil. Such was their emotional involvement with the game that nine million Dutch fans, 60 per cent of the population, partied on the streets after the final whistle – the largest public gathering since the liberation.

Across the country delirious Dutchmen reportedly carried their bicycles in the air like trophies, because the occupying Germans had confiscated them during the war. Anti-German feelings were clearly running high, and it wasn't just felt in the Netherlands: at the post-match press conference, coach Rinus Michels, he who coined the phrase 'football is war', was given a standing ovation by 150 foreign journalists. The following day goalkeeper Jan Jongbloed sent the side a telegram on behalf of the 1974 team. It simply read: '*We have been released from our suffering.*'

The Dutch went on to win the final against the Soviet Union, with goals from Gullit and an epic van Basten volley, but it was no secret that the semi-final was the grudge match of the tournament. Goalkeeper Hans van Breukelen had been waiting for this moment for 14 years: "Before the game I remembered my feelings watching TV as a teenager, and that boosted my anger. I'm happy to have been able to give this gift to the older generation, the ones who lived through the war."

Ruud Gullit was equally elated: "We gave joy to the older generation. I saw their emotion and their tears."

When the triumphant Dutch side returned home, Michels addressed the nation in front of the Dutch Royal Palace in Amsterdam: "We won the tournament but we all know that the semi-final was the real final."

The match marked a watershed in the relationship between the two countries. Whereas before the Dutch had dwelled on the injustice of the wartime occupation, they believed the semi-final victory went some way to consigning that period to history, and they now saw the Germans only as intense football rivals. Sensing that the atmosphere had changed, the war largely forgotten, the Germans became far more vocal in their football-based rivalry because they knew the teams were now viewed as equally competitive.

Holland and Germany were drawn in the same qualifying group for the 1990 World Cup, with both fixtures ending in stalemate. These games did little to assuage the bad blood – on and off the pitch – between the teams and the shift in attitude was confirmed when the sides met in the second round of the tournament proper in Italy. This game undoubtedly marked the moment when the rivalry assumed its modern significance.

The Dutch booed the German anthem in Milan's San Siro Stadium, and the Germans replied with anti-Dutch chants. The match that followed would prove combative and controversial in equal measure. Approaching the midpoint of the first half, Frank Rijkaard was first booked for a foul on Rudi Völler, before going one step further by spitting in the German striker's hair. After the free kick, Völler clashed with goalkeeper Hans van

Breukelen. Rijkaard intervened, shouting at Völler and then pulling his hair. When the referee sent the pair off, Rijkaard once again spat at the German. There were riots along the border between the countries. Rijkaard was a mild-mannered footballer with tremendous talent, so it was inexplicable that he should resort to such behaviour. He apologised after the match, saying that what he had done was inexcusable. Although many claimed that Völler had racially abused him, Rijkaard has always defended the German and takes full responsibility for the incident.

Although Völler wasn't entirely innocent, the Germans clearly felt hard done by. At half-time they resolved to win the game on his behalf. With Rijkaard also off, Jürgen Klinsmann found he had much more space up front and, set up by Guido Buchwald, he opened the scoring with a smart left-footed finish. He almost scored again shortly afterwards but his fierce right-foot shot ricocheted off the post. The match remained bad tempered however, with both sides committing some terrible late tackles. After more solid work from Buchwald, Andreas Brehme finally silenced the Dutch resistance with a glorious shot from the edge of the area with five minutes left.

Despite the Dutch pulling a goal back with a late Koeman penalty after van Basten's theatrical tumble, Germany went on to win the match 2-1. Under coach Franz Beckenbauer they would eventually lift the World Cup by beating Argentina in the final, exacting revenge for their Maradona-inspired defeat in the final four years earlier.

The balance of power seemed to be shifting once again. But, having waited for two years to avenge this latest defeat, the Dutch lined up against the Germans in the group stages of Euro '92 in Denmark. Ten million people watched the game in Holland, a new record for a television audience.

Rijkaard opened the scoring with a looping header from a Koeman free kick: two German fans threw a homemade bomb into a nightclub in Kerkrade. Rob Witschge made it 2-0 with a low drive from 35 yards that took a slight deflection and crept in off the post: Dutch and German fans rioted along the border at Enschede. Van Basten almost made it 3-0 but his superb left-foot volley from outside the box rebounded off the crossbar.

Although Klinsmann pulled one back with a bullet header from close range, Dennis Bergkamp made it 3-1 late on with a beautifully angled header into the bottom corner: five hundred Dutch fans invaded the German town of Gronau. This was as close to war as things got these days.

The Dutch looked like the form team of the tournament, but they hadn't counted on the hosts exceeding all expectations and the Danes won a penalty shootout in the semi-final before going on to ambush the Germans in the final. Of course the Danes had also been occupied in the war, so their fans sent the Germans packing with rousing renditions of *Auf Wiedersehen, Deutschland!*

The Dutch failed to qualify for the 2002 World Cup in the Far East – when the Germans made the final yet again – so the next competitive Holland-Germany meeting was in the group stages of Euro 2004 in Portugal. It turned out to be a relatively tame affair and finished 1-1. Surprisingly, given that most of this team had reached the previous World Cup final, this was a poor tournament for the Germans and they failed to win a match. The Dutch, however, made it to the semi-final where they were beaten by the hosts.

The last meeting between the two was again during the high-stakes group stages of the 2012 European Championships in Ukraine. Germany raced into a two-goal lead thanks to a Mario Gomez brace, and, despite Holland pulling a goal back after a superb Robin van Persie finish, it was to no avail. The Dutch would soon be packing their bags, while Germany went on to reach the semi-final.

Although their 40 meetings have yielded 15 victories for Germany and 10 for Holland, Germany have won six major titles to Holland's one, so there's no doubt which team holds the sporting high ground. However good the Dutch sides are they can't seem to convert final places into winners' medals, as evidenced by their showing in the 2010 World Cup final against Spain in South Africa. Aware that they couldn't live with the crisp passing and incisive movement of the Spanish, the Dutch decided to disrupt the Spanish with ferocious tackling instead – a world away from the attitude of the 1974 World Cup team. Had referee Howard Webb and his assistants seen all of the challenges, he would surely have sent several Dutch players from the field.

German television was quick to jump on the Dutch defeat and was quite happy to show their fans in tears. Of course this was only in retaliation at the Dutch broadcasters showing distraught German fans after their defeat by Spain in the other semi-final.

In the words of the great Johnny Rep: "It shouldn't need explaining. It may be getting less heated but that rivalry will always stay."

Verdict: Although the Dutch have scored some notable victories over the years, Germany are historically the stronger team and have won five more tournaments. Both sides are now amongst the world's elite but Germany remain favourites whenever the two sides clash.

Alain Prost

vs

Ayrton Senna

Since Ayrton Senna's death at Imola in 1994, he has been consistently voted as one of the world's finest racing drivers. Most experts agree that he stands alongside Fangio, Clark and Schumacher at the top of a distinguished pile. But greatness can only be accurately measured when compared with other greats from your era, and, in Nigel Mansell and Nelson Piquet, Senna found himself up against tough and talented competition. It is his rivalry with Alain Prost, however, that defines their careers – Senna the uncompromising but flawed genius, Prost the meticulous professional. How Formula 1 today could do with a rivalry as bitter and compelling.

Ayrton Senna da Silva was born in São Paulo, Brazil, in March 1960. The family were wealthy business people and landowners, and his father, a motorsport enthusiast, presented the young Ayrton with a tiny lawnmower engine-powered kart when he was only four. Initially awkward and with a lack of focus, Senna suddenly found something that interested him, but Brazilian law prevented him from racing until his 13th birthday. His first race at the Interlagos kart complex was against talented local prospects, but Senna won and the legend was born.

Four years later he won the first of two South American Kart Championships, before heading to Europe for the World Championships at Le Mans, where he finished a respectable sixth against seasoned drivers with far more experience. He arrived in England in 1981 to drive for Ralph Firman's Van Diemen team in the Formula Ford Championship, and he promptly won both of the series he was contesting.

There were several Brazilian drivers looking for places in the higher formulas in the early '80s and, as Senna didn't have financial backing to help the teams, he was overlooked. He decided to retire and return to Brazil to work for his father. He immediately regretted the decision, talked his father into sponsoring him and returned to England to win 22 races and the 1982 championship. Formula 3 was the next step, but Martin Brundle would provide a stern test during the 1983 season. The Englishman was one of the first to appreciate Senna's incredible skill, but he was also the first to feel the pressure Senna piled on you if you were racing him wheel to wheel: "He made you believe that he would rather have an accident than yield to you. He had this obsession to win at all costs."

Senna won the final race and took the title, which immediately caught the attention of Formula 1 team bosses. Brabham expressed an interest but Nelson Piquet blocked Senna's move, so the Brazilian took the only remaining option and joined Toleman, a second-tier team that was unlikely to help him achieve good results. His first few outings were dogged by mechanical failures and poor finishes, but he somehow managed to qualify 13th for the Monaco Grand Prix. Senna was already making a name for himself as a superb wet-weather racer and the heavens opened soon after the start.

With more experienced drivers making mistakes, Senna gradually carved his way through the field and by lap seven he was up to sixth place. He continued pushing hard and when Mansell and Lauda both span out Senna found himself in second, 34 seconds behind Alain Prost. Eleven laps later he was only seven seconds adrift, a quite remarkable drive considering the man ahead and the conditions. With the rain pouring down, Senna eventually overtook the Frenchman but the organisers stopped the race on the same lap, thus denying the young Brazilian a debut victory (the last full lap completed by all the drivers was deemed to be the end of the race).

His performances and ninth place in the World Championship had piqued the interest of Lotus, however, and he

155

signed for them the following season. Now that he had a competitive car, Senna was ready to challenge for the greatest prize in motorsport.

Alain Marie Pascal Prost was born near St-Étienne, France, in February 1955. Young Alain was always destined to be short but his height didn't stop him developing into a footballer of considerable talent. Having tried karting at the age of 14 however, Prost hung up his boots and devoted his attention to motorsport.

He soon showed his talent for karting by winning several championships, and he left school in 1974 to pursue the sport full-time. He won the 1975 Senior French Championship and earned a place in Formula Renault as a result. He won this series twice and the French and European Formula 3 titles in 1979. By now he was hot property and several Formula 1 teams tried to secure his signature. McLaren offered him a drive in the last race of the 1979 season at Watkins Glen, but he surprised everyone and turned it down because he knew he wasn't fully prepared. He valued their offer so highly, however, that he signed for the 1980 season anyway.

His first full year in the top formula was a mixed bag of low points finishes, mechanical failures and accidents, some of which McLaren blamed on their young driver. Prost was not impressed with the car's reliability and broke his contract to move to Renault alongside fellow Frenchman René Arnoux.

Although the all-French team looked perfect on paper, Arnoux was immediately wary of his supremely talented team-mate and couldn't stop the young driver winning three races, including his first at his home grand prix. Prost went on to finish fifth in the championship just seven points behind world champion Nelson Piquet.

The following year Prost won two more races and came fourth in the championship, but his relationship with Arnoux and the French press had reached rock bottom. Something had to give, and it was Arnoux who left the team. Prost promptly won four races in the 1983 season and only missed out on the overall championship because he felt the team had been too conservative towards the end of the season. Renault disagreed and fired him immediately. Prost was promptly re-hired by a resurgent McLaren.

Although Senna's star was on the rise, Prost was now with the best team and driving one of the best cars and he dominated the 1984 season, winning seven races and only losing out on the overall championship to team-mate Niki Lauda by a half point (half points were awarded for the black-flagged Monaco Grand Prix that Senna nearly won). The following year, 1985, Prost won five more races and became the first French World Champion.

Despite being behind on points before the last race of the 1986 season in Australia, championship favourite Nigel Mansell had a high-speed blow-out and team-mate Nelson Piquet pitted for new tyres as a precaution. Prost drove a problem-free race and successfully defended his title. In 1987 he overtook Jackie Stewart's record of 27 F1 victories, but his car was a little off the pace and he finished the season in fourth place.

Senna, meanwhile, was slowly building on a positive start at Lotus. He won the 1985 Portuguese GP, his first, in torrential rain, then backed it up with seven pole positions, two podium finishes and a win at Spa. He finished fourth in the championship won by Prost, but his searing pole position laps hinted at the greatness to come. He also performed well in 1986 and was leading the championship until poor reliability saw him fall behind Mansell, Piquet and eventual champion Prost.

Lotus secured a deal with engine manufacturer Honda for 1987 and Senna started the season strongly. However, the Williams cars of Piquet and Mansell were too strong and he eventually finished the season in third, one place ahead of Prost. The Frenchman was so impressed with Senna's driving that he convinced McLaren team principle Ron Dennis to hire him as the number two driver for 1988. Senna had a great relationship with Honda, so McLaren got the best engine as part of the deal. All the pieces were in place and the stage was set for the most dangerous and controversial rivalry in the history of sport.

Senna took pole in the first race of the 1988 season at Interlagos, but mechanical failure forced him out and allowed Prost to take the chequered flag. McLaren also dominated at Imola with the turbo-powered cars lapping the entire field. This time Senna took the win with Prost in second. Senna out-qualified the more conservative Prost by over a second in Monaco, but Prost drove an inspired race and set the fastest lap. Senna was so determined to beat his time that he crashed into the wall before the tunnel and handed his team-mate victory. It was his lowest point so far in Formula 1 and he fled to an apartment in the principality to dwell on his error.

It was then that Prost sensed a change Senna's attitude towards him: "You cannot compare Ayrton with a normal driver. I don't know exactly when it happened but I gradually realised that his motivation was not just to beat me but to destroy me."

The two traded pole positions and race wins (apart from at Monza, where both McLarens retired, ruining a perfect season) before the Belgian Grand Prix at Spa. Senna had copied Prost's aerodynamic settings for all of the previous races and Prost was annoyed that the Brazilian had scored six wins to his four. So he changed his settings at the last minute. The plan backfired however, and Senna won comfortably.

The underlying mistrust came to a head at the Portuguese Grand Prix in September. Prost took pole but Senna got away more cleanly and led the first lap. Prost then pulled out to overtake on the pit straight, but Senna couldn't bear to yield and barged Prost towards the pit wall at full speed. Prost showed great bravery and kept his foot down and, with Senna having mechanical problems late on, he held on for victory, although angry words were exchanged between the two afterwards. The FIA stepped in and warned Senna for dangerous driving and he eventually apologised to Prost. The peace had been kept, just.

The 1988 championship was decided at Suzuka in Japan. Senna stalled on the grid and handed Prost the advantage but it soon began to rain. Prost was notoriously cautious in the wet, but Senna was even more aggressive than usual and he took the chequered flag. The title followed despite Prost outscoring him by 11 points – in those days only a driver's best 11 race results from the 16 rounds counted, so Senna's eight wins and three seconds trumped Prost's seven wins and four seconds.

The relationship between the two deteriorated during the winter, but McLaren insisted they both continue racing for the team in 1989. It was probably a decision they regretted. Gerhard Berger had a huge crash at Imola early in the season and the San

Marino Grand Prix had to be stopped. Senna overtook Prost at the restart, which incensed the Frenchman as he claimed the move violated a pre-race agreement between them. He then refused to speak with or about the Brazilian before the next race at Monaco.

The two men traded wins at Mexico, France, Britain and Germany, but by the Italian Grand Prix at Monza it was clear that Prost's relationship with McLaren and Senna was beyond repair and the Frenchman announced he would be driving for Ferrari the following year. Senna retired from the lead late in the race itself and Prost took the chequered flag. He then gave the trophy to the hordes of *tifosi* (Italian Ferrari fans) to signal his intent for 1990. Ron Dennis was so disappointed that he threw the winning constructors' trophy at Prost's feet and stormed off the podium.

Matters came to one of several heads at the Japanese Grand Prix at Suzuka. Senna started from pole but made a poor start and Prost took the lead. He was so comfortable that he even claimed to slow down deliberately just so that he could pull ahead from a battling Senna. To the thousands of fans at the circuit and hundreds of millions watching on television it was an epic duel between two men at the peak of their powers.

Prost knew that Senna would not give up if he beat the Brazilian off the line, but he also warned his team-mate that he would not stand for any dangerous passing attempts or reckless driving. Senna, of course, needed no encouragement to test Prost's nerve. However, it took until the 47th lap before he made his move.

From a long way behind the rival McLaren, Senna roared up the inside at the chicane before the start / finish straight. Prost didn't initially see him but, when his team-mate's car filled his wing mirror, he calmly turned in for the corner, instead, as most drivers would have done, of yielding to the overly aggressive pass.

The cars collided and both slid into the escape road opposite and stalled. Prost shook his head and climbed out of his car. Senna was not giving up, however. He knew that with Prost out he could still contest the championship by winning the race. He urged the marshals to give him a push start and then weaved through the escape road to rejoin the circuit. Having pitted for repairs, he then drove like a man possessed and overtook Alessandro Nannini's Benetton at the chicane two laps from the end to take the chequered flag.

Prost initially thought he'd made a mistake by not urging the marshals to help him too, but the rules stated that they were not allowed to push a car and Senna had also missed the chicane. As he hadn't officially completed that lap he was disqualified and Prost was declared World Champion. Senna was outraged and immediately launched an appeal, but the stewards refused to give an inch and the result stood. In fact, the FIA ended up charging Senna with endangering other drivers, gave him a suspended six-month driving ban and fined him $100,000. Even Prost was surprised by the severity of the punishment, perhaps because he felt a little guilty for turning into the chicane a fraction early and making sure the two cars touched... We may never know.

The last race of the season was at a rain-soaked Adelaide. Prost, now confirmed as champion, refused to race in appalling conditions. An angry Senna went out to prove a point and started driving, according to Martin Brundle, like a complete idiot. With Brundle easing off so he could see through the blinding spray on the Brabham straight, Senna careered into the back of his car at full speed. It was an inglorious end to an eventful season.

Prost had already left for the airport, but he was increasingly unhappy with Senna's behaviour: "When you want to be the best, you need to have a challenge from a rival, but you can't have enemies. Senna had made me an enemy, but I was not prepared to lose my life in a battle with another driver."

During the winter preceding the 1990 championship, Senna was racking up more enemies, this time in the shape of Jean-Marie Balestre, the French President of the FIA. He hadn't paid his fine and accused Balestre of ruling in favour of Prost after the collision at Suzuka. Balestre then threatened not to renew his super licence unless he apologised and paid the fine, and he also cited Senna for dangerous driving at five races in the previous two years.

The Brazilian promptly won the first race in Phoenix, but then refused to shake Prost's hand afterwards. The Formula 1 circus then moved on to Senna's home grand prix in São Paulo. He took pole and built up a commanding lead before colliding with a back marker. The unscheduled pitstop allowed Prost through to take the chequered flag, his first win for Ferrari. The mood within the Italian team was changing, however. Prost and Mansell had initially been comfortable with one another, but Mansell believed Prost was now getting favourable treatment, and Prost thought Mansell paranoid and too involved with his golfing commitments.

Tension throughout the grid was rising as the teams arrived in Portugal. Mansell took pole with Prost alongside and Senna just behind. The Ferraris started badly, however, and Senna stormed through to take the lead. Mansell drove an inspired race and managed to slip past Senna, but the Frenchman couldn't find a way around the Brazilian and had to settle for third, a position he believes cost him that year's championship.

He still managed to win in Spain the following week and cut Senna's championship lead to nine points. Then the drivers headed back to Japan for what would become the title decider. Senna drove like a man possessed and snatched pole position, and he then asked to start from the left hand side of the grid, which was on the racing line and therefore cleaner. His request was denied and Prost made the better start. Senna was having none of it and kept his foot down into the first corner. Prost turned in to clip the apex only to find Senna's McLaren bearing down on him at full tilt. The cars collided and bounced off into the gravel on the outside of the corner.

It was a foolish move and there was no way Senna could have made the corner at that speed. Most observers believed he had won the championship by deliberately taking Prost out and avenging the collision from the previous year, which he still considered Prost's fault. Prost returned to his garage incandescent with rage that someone could have risked both their lives – and the lives of more than 20 drivers behind all with full fuel tanks – to have a 160mph crash. He said he had wanted to get out of the car and punch Senna but couldn't bring himself to do it. "I thought he was a member of the human race, that he was hard but fair. If it is not possible to apply sanctions against this type of driving, then I may not continue racing. I'm not ready to fight against irresponsible people who are not afraid to die."

Senna dismissed Prost's comments out of hand: "I don't give a damn what he says. I cannot be responsible for his actions. He moved over on me, as usual. He has tried to destroy me but he will not succeed."

Senna took his third world championship the following year in a largely controversy-free season, although the pair almost came to blows during the German Grand Prix, when Senna aggressively defended fourth place and forced the Frenchman into the escape road. Prost's Ferrari was not a serious challenger, however, and Senna landed seven wins. He also finally came clean about the accident at Suzuka: "Balestre's decision to change the position of the pole sitter to the dirty side of the track was unquestionably unfair so I refused to yield the corner to Prost. If he decided to take the racing line, there would be an accident."

For Prost, this only confirmed what he already knew: "It was a disgusting move. He is a man without value."

Due to contractual wranglings and team politics, Prost ended up taking a sabbatical from the sport in 1992. He returned in 1993 with Willams and promptly won his fourth world title. Again, his biggest challenge came from Senna in an under-powered McLaren, but the two managed to avoid major incident. Senna then found out that Prost had blocked his move to the Williams team, so he labelled the Frenchman a coward and mocked the team's association with gaming giant SEGA by sticking a squashed hedgehog logo on the nose of his McLaren. Prost needed the services of a security team at most races to protect him from the hordes of Brazilian fans.

When Prost announced his retirement at the end of the season, Senna no longer saw him as a rival and embraced him on the podium at Adelaide, a gesture that initially surprised the Frenchman. It marked another turning point in their relationship, because both men suddenly realised that they had become the great drivers and sporting personalities of that era because of their rivalry. Indeed, it can be said with some certainty that their epic duels defined motorsport in the 1980s and early 1990s.

With Senna feeling unfulfilled and aching for someone to

challenge him, he repeatedly telephoned Prost to beg him to come out of retirement. Prost was again surprised by the Brazilian's tactics, but grew to understand that Senna was only the man he was because Prost had given meaning to his career and a purpose to his life.

No one will know if this more tolerant acceptance of one another would have developed into genuine friendship because Senna was killed at Imola early in the 1994 season. The maverick genius was gone and the racing world went into shock. Three million people – the largest such gathering in modern history – lined the streets of São Paulo to pay their respects. Alain Prost was one of the pallbearers at the funeral.

Verdict: Aficionados will argue that with a win ratio of 25 per cent (he won a quarter of the F1 races he started) and a greater number of pole positions Senna was the finer driver, and there's no doubt that he took more risks. But purists will say that Prost (whose win ratio was practically identical) won more races overall, and more titles, and he was a smoother, cleaner driver.

An interesting comparison can be made between Jenson Button and Lewis Hamilton, the former smooth and accurate, the latter bold and unpredictable. Who can decide which man is better, or faster, when their statistics are so closely matched? The pure joy that Senna found at the wheel was intoxicating to watch, especially in such a short career, but this does not necessarily make him the best driver. Too close to call.

List of sporting rivalries

Andrew's choices	Liam's choices
15. The Boat Race	The Boat Race
14. Fischer vs Spassky	Fischer vs Spassky
13. State of Origin	State of Origin
12. Thompson vs Hingsen	Thompson vs Hingsen
11. Borg vs McEnroe	Borg vs McEnroe
10. Evert vs Navratilova	Nicklaus vs Palmer
9. Bird vs Johnson	The Ashes
8. Holland vs Germany	Evert vs Navratilova
7. Nicklaus vs Palmer	Bird vs Johnson
6. The Ashes	Ovett vs Coe
5. Ovett vs Coe	The Fantastic Four
4. The Fantastic Four	The Ryder Cup
3. The Ryder Cup	Holland Germany
2. Prost vs Senna	Prost vs Senna
1. Ali vs Frazier	Ali vs Frazier

Andrew can be contacted via Twitter at: @Bettys_dad

Liam can be contacted via Twitter at: @liambmccann or through his website: www.liambmccann.com

Printed in Great Britain
by Amazon.co.uk, Ltd.,
Marston Gate.